Intr

There are codes in the Hebrew Torah. These codes have been mathematically proven to exist. The codes are found through Equidistant Letter Sequences (ELS).
For example, Instead of reading a text normally—one letter at a time—hidden words are looked for by reading the text every 2, or 3, or 4, (etc.), letters, skipping over the letters in between.
For example, we will use the name, Joan Coombs. If we were to read this at every two letter skips, it would read "J-a-c-o-b."

This is a very simple illustration to give you an idea of how the codes are found. The actual Bible codes are far more complex as they can be found forwards, backward, and diagonal. Several of the codes repeat themselves over and over.
Several people that have studied the Bible codes over the years have been searching for the "code key". A key that will unlock the secrets to what they think is an infinite amount of information that reveals all the mysteries of the universe, from the beginning to the end of time and beyond.

There has never been verifiable evidence as to where this code originated, how it works, and exactly how much information it contains......until now!

Chapter 1
The Torah

"The rule is that all that was, is, and will be, unto the end of time is included in the Torah, from the first word to the last word. And not merely in a general sense, but as to the details of every species and each one individually, and details of details of everything that happened to him from the day of his birth until his end."

-Rabbi Elijah Ben Solomon Zalman (1722-1797)

There are dark powers that work behind the scenes to try and prevent people from stepping outside of what they have been told in school or heard through main-stream media. People tend to dismiss offhand anything that goes against what they have been conditioned to believe, regardless of the evidence that supports some of these claims. These dark powers know that people will jump at any chance to dismiss information that goes against the status quo.

Therefore, it doesn't take much solid evidence for these powers to claim to have debunked whatever info goes against the status quo since people are already looking for any excuse to dismiss this information and get back to their comfort zone of status quo life.

The Bible codes are no exception to this and there are several sites that claim to have debunked the Bible codes. They claim that words can be found in just about any book through ELS. There is some truth to this as you can find simple words and occasionally word combinations in most large books, however, these debunk sites are just disinformation to mislead the masses.

One of the main books they will reference is the classic Moby Dick.

Though Moby Dick does contain some impressive word combinations due to its size and the statistical odds that come with this size, it in no way, shape, or form debunks or compares to the Bible codes.

So what's the difference? The Bible codes contain all information, from the beginning until the end of space-time, that exist in our known universe. I realize that this is a profound statement but In the following pages, I will explain why this is true and how it works.
So buckle up as we take this journey deep into the rabbit hole.

How deep are we talking here? This journey will reveal some of the most amazing evidence proving God that has ever been discovered by man. Even the most devout atheist will be forced to admit God is real or go into complete denial of the facts.

Since the Torah is the spoken word of God, this path to solving the Bible code will unlock the deep mysteries of creation down to the finest details and conclude by showing you where God's literal Word is, what His voice sounds like, and where you can go to literally hear and recognize His audible voice anytime you want to for the first time in history.

I realize this is a bold statement but the evidence will speak for itself, literally, and prove what I am claiming.

I know that at this point several readers will be tempted to skip to the end of the book and search for this evidence. Please resist the urge to do this as it is critical that you take this journey with me before you can totally appreciate the ending conclusions.

First, I think we should address the origin of the Torah Codes. Obviously, the Torah codes are found in the Torah.

Biblical history tells us that Moses copied the Torah directly from the mouth of God.

Since that time the Torah has been copied by scribes, word for word and letter for letter identical to the one transcribed by Moses as God dictated it.

So the first record of the Torah written by man as God dictated came from Moses, however this is not where the Torah originated.

That statement alone could give some of you who are reading this, and very knowledgeable in Torah studies, the urge to set this book aside now and find a better way to spend your time.

The true origin of the Torah is much more profound and amazing and I promise it will be well worth your time to look at the evidence as it is presented in the pages to come.

One of the clues that point us to the origin of the Torah is the command that is given to the scribes.

"Even to this day, a Torah scroll is copied by hand from it's predecessor, written out according to unchanging rules, by scribes who undergo an exact detail course of training and preparation. To each of them the following warning has been passed down through the ages; Should you perchance omit or add one single letter from the Torah, you would thereby destroy all the universe."

Most people would assume that this statement Is an exaggeration to put emphasis on how important it is not to make any mistakes when copying the Torah. The mind-bending fact of the matter is that this is not an exaggeration and if we take it seriously we will have our first clue on the path to solving the Bible code.

If a mistake in copying the Torah is equal to destroying the universe and we take this statement at face value then the Torah must have a direct and vitally important connection to the formation of the universe.

We know the Torah is the spoken word of God so lets see what God's word has to say about this.

Hebrews 11:3 KJV

Through faith we understand that the worlds were framed by the word of God, so that things which are seen were not made of things which do appear.

This is just one of several verses that reveals the location of God's word. God's word frames or surrounds the universe.

This verse is also one of many verses in the Bible that go into quantum physics.

Things we see, the physical, are made of things that we can't see, the quantum world of protons, electrons, and neutrons etc.

You can't appreciate, or even discover, a lot of the areas that the Bible gives the details of regarding quantum physics and how it works until you come to the correct conclusions on exactly what the plaintext is saying.

There are several areas that either haven't been addressed by the church or have been addressed, but they came to the wrong conclusions and shouted it out to the world for years and hence have several people believing something that is either partially true or totally false in extreme cases.

One good example of this is the belief that the New Jerusalem is in the shape of a giant cube.

I wrote an entire chapter in The Matrix Code and The Alien Agenda that proves beyond any doubt that the shape of the New Jerusalem is a pyramid. For the sake of those that read my other books I won't rehash all the information again but I will explain how the cube conclusion was mistakenly reached and why it's critical to look at each and every word a verse says in context before drawing any conclusions.

The description of New Jerusalem states that "the city lieth foursquare, and the length is as large the breadth: and he measured the city with the reed, twelve thousand furlongs. The length and the breadth and the height of it are equal."

The key to understanding the true shape lays within the details of the description in context. "the city LIETH foursquare" It is making reference to the base or the part that "lays" on the ground. A pyramid "lieth" foursquare, but a cube is squared regardless of if you are talking about the top, side or bottom.

A pyramid is also the same length, width, and height in keeping with the measurements given in scripture.

Keep in mind that Christ is the chief head stone that the builders rejected.

Matthew 21:42
Jesus saith unto them, Did ye never read in the

scriptures, The stone which the builders rejected, the same is become the head of the corner: this is the Lord's doing, and it is marvellous in our eyes?

Psalm 118:22

The stone which the builders refused is become the head stone of the corner.

Mark 12:10

And have ye not read this scripture; The stone which the builders rejected is become the head of the corner:

We know that "head" makes reference to the top or capstone and we know that all four corners of a pyramid meet at the head or capstone. Making the capstone the head of the corners.

We know the New Jerusalem represents the Bride and body of Christ which is the church. Jesus is the Head of the church, or head stone, which would be the shape of a pyramid.

Once we understand the shape that represents Jesus Christ we can unlock verses that reveal the secrets of quantum physics.

For example, recent studies in quantum physics indicate that smallest shape in our reality is a pyramid that we know represents Jesus Christ who is the Head of the church.

A Planck Length is the smallest division of matter at the quantum level and the first shape it will end up forming is a tetrahedron. In other words the pyramid shape comes before all other physical matter and is the "building block" that all physcal matter starts with.

With that in mind let's take a look at quantum physics in the Bible.

Colossians 1:16-20 (KJV)

16 For by him were all things created, that are in heaven, and that are in earth, visible and invisible, whether they be thrones, or dominions, or principalities, or powers: all things were created by him, and for him:

17 And he is before all things, and by him all things consist.

18 And he is the head of the body, the church: who is the beginning, the firstborn from the dead; that in all things he might have the preeminence.

There you go. Christ is before all things (the Planck Length comes before all other matter) and then it goes on to give the pyramid shape when it states that Christ is the Head (pyramid shaped capstone) of the body (the New Jerusalem or church) who is the beginning.

However, our reality is temporary, and passing away, according to the Bible, and Jesus Christ is eternal. Everything in our reality is just a dim mirror reflection of eternity.

1 Corinthians 13:12 NLT

Now we see things imperfectly, like puzzling reflections in a mirror, but then we will see

everything with perfect clarity. All that I know now is partial and incomplete, but then I will know everything completely, just as God now knows me completely.

This means that the tetrahedron is just a temporary mirror reflection of the eternal makeup of Jesus Christ. As 1 Corinthians 13:12 states, what we see in this reality is partial and incomplete. The tetrahedron i partial and incomplete. It is missing the fourth side at the base.

The base of a tetrahedron only has three sides and the eternal head stone shape that represents Jesus Christ has a four-sided base, yet both are pyramids.

When you look in the mirror you cannot see the bottom of your feet. When you look at a tetrahedron in the mirror you cannot see beneath it, or its base, you can only see the face which is a triangle. When you look at the face of the pyramid shape that represents Jesus Christ in a mirror you will see the same exact shape, a triangle.

This is where things get really interesting. If you combine two tetrahedrons at the quantum level you get what we could refer to as the first quantum building block beyond the pyramid shape in our reality. When you connect all the outside points you get a hexagon.

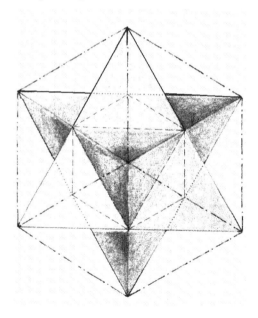

A hexagon has six sides and we can see it in natural formations such as the honycomb in a beehive. There is strong evidence supporting this as one of the foundational building blocks in our reality. It's as if the inner atomic structure of gas giant planets is projected to the poles.

If we take a look at the poles on Saturn and Neptune we will find the hexagon shape. Infrared instruments see Saturn by the thermal radiation emitted from its interior, and they have been getting fantastic views of the hexagon.

The following is a photo of Saturn's north pole that was originally discovered during the Voyager flybys of Saturn in the 1980s.

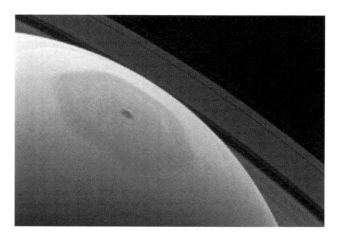

SATURN

The number 6 refers to earthly matters, and you can find naturally occurring instances of 6 in magnified photos of water crystals and snowflakes. Slice open a tomato or bell pepper and you often find six chambers. Honey combs are shaped as 6-sided hexagons.

In the Bible, the number 6 symbolizes man and human weakness, the evils of Satan and the manifestation of sin. Man was created on the sixth day. Men are appointed 6 days to labor.

The sixth commandment prohibits the murder of man and the supposed unholy trinity of the beast and his number is 666 so this is why it is sometimes referred to as an unholy trinity and as such the bringing together of three 6's is the

number and mark of the end time Beast of Revelation.

Revelation 13:18 NLT

Wisdom is needed here. Let the one with understanding solve the meaning of the number of the beast, for it is the number of a man. His number is 666.

So we can see that the number 6 prevails in this temporary fallen universe that we live in and 666 is the number of the beast, or Antichrist, who is Satan in the flesh.

This is just another example of Satan putting his evil twist on something God has done in order to try and replicate Jesus Christ and thereby deceive mankind.

Let's do a quick review.

The tetrahedron is a pyramid with a three-sided base that is a mirror image of Jesus Christ who represents the pyramid shape with a four sided base, which is a quadrilateral pyramid.

The first quantum building block we get by combining two tetrahedrons has six points and is hexagonal. Jesus comes before all reality and holds all reality together.

Colossians 1:17 ESV

And he is before all things, and in him all things hold together.

The hexagon is derived from the tetrahedron and is just the mirror image of Christ.

 It represents a temporary reality that is passing away and fallen. It also represents 6, the number of man. Man was created in the image of God.

Genesis 1:27 KJV

So God created man in his own image, in the image of God created he him; male and female created he them.

If we wanted an exact representation of Jesus Christ as the Head Stone or the Head of the church, we would get a pyramid with a four-sided base, or a quadrilateral pyramid.

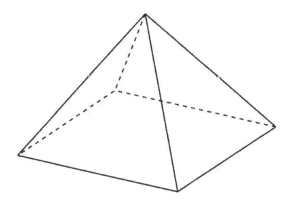

If we combine two quadrilateral pyramids we will get the first quantum building block for an eternal reality.

It has eight sides. If you connect the edges you will get an octagon.

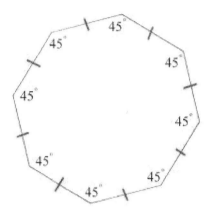

The
octagon stands for;

Regeneration

Totality

Infinity

Rebirth

We are Regenerated through Jesus Christ.

2 Corinthians 5:17 KJV

Therefore if any man be in Christ, he is a new creature: old things are passed away; behold, all things are become new.

Jesus Christ is the totality of all existence.

Colossians 1:17 ESV

And he is before all things, and in him all things hold together.

Jesus is infinite.

Revelation 1:8 KJV

I am Alpha and Omega, the beginning and the ending, saith the Lord, which is, and which was, and which is to come, the Almighty.

Jesus gives us spiritual Rebirth.

John 3:3 KJV

Jesus answered and said unto him, Verily, verily, I say unto thee, Except a man be born again, he cannot see the kingdom of God.

Interestingly, the two overlapping squares form what is know as the Seal, or Signet of Melchizedek.

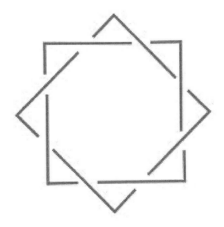

"The Signet of Melchizedek, King of Righteousness and Priest of the Most High God; King of Schalaam, which is King of Peace-the Octalpha or eight fold endless triangle, which, being a geometric figure composed of lines continually reproduced to infinity, by right angles, horizontals, perpendiculars and diagonals, was hailed by our ancient brethern among all nations, as the symbol of the Divine Omnipotence, Omniscience and Omnipresence; universal, infinite and eternal."

This seal has been taken over and abused by several pagan religions but it was originally mentioned in Psalm 110:1- 4 as an example of Jesus Christ being our priest forever.

Psalm 110:1- 4 KJV

1The Lord said unto my Lord, Sit thou at my right hand, until I make thine enemies thy footstool.

2 The Lord shall send the rod of thy strength out of Zion: rule thou in the midst of thine enemies.

3 Thy people shall be willing in the day of thy power, in the beauties of holiness from the womb of the morning: thou hast the dew of thy youth.

4 *The Lord hath sworn, and will not repent, Thou art a priest for ever after the order of Melchizedek.*

Lastly, I want to point out that the number of Jesus is 888!

Using the Greek Ionic Ciphered Numeral System scientifically proves this. In this system, each letter of the Greek alphabet is assigned a numerical value. The name of Jesus in Greek is spelled I H S O U S (iota, eta, sigma, omicron, upsilon, sigma). Substituting in the Greek numeral system the equivalent numerical values to each letter in the name of Jesus and adding them up, the total is 888. The values of each letter are: iota, 10; eta, 8; sigma, 200; omicron, 70; upsilon, 400; sigma, 200. The sum of 10 + 8 + 200 + 70 + 400 + 200 is 888.

Now we can understand why the tetrahedron is an incomplete and temporary mirror reflection representing our current reality and the eternal

pyramid shape with a square base represents Jesus Christ at the quantum level of an eternal reality.

If you are a doubter and think this is scripture out of context, I can prove this point as it is verified throughout the Bible.

We know the Bible says Jesus is the Word and we just went quantum showing that Jesus is "the beginning." He is "before all things, and by him all things consist." Jesus represents the first shape, or building block in our reality after the Planck Length, which is a tetrahedron or pyramid (head; capstone) when we are at the quantum level.

Let's give another example.

John 1-4 (KJV)

1 In the beginning was the Word, and the Word was with God, and the Word was God.

2 The same was in the beginning with God.

3 All things were made by him; and without him was not any thing made that was made.

4 In him was life; and the life was the light of men.

Not only does **John 1-4** repeat what we just verified in Colossians 1:16-20, but it goes on to say " In him was life; and the life was the light of men."

Starting with the Planck Length, everything in the universe starts with, is held together by, and consist of light. Light is literally what forms and gives life at the quantum level.

 Our universe started with a sudden explosion of light.

Genesis 1:3

And God said, Let there be light: and there was light.

The hidden light	אר הגנוז	Its light is the ancient light	אורו אור ישן
Menorah	מנורה		

Chapter 2
An Explosion of Light; The Big Bang

"And God said, Let there be light: and there was light."
-God in **Genesis 1:3 KJV**

When God said "Let there be light" there was an explosion of light. This was the beginning of our known universe and it resembles a "Big Bang". However, this does not support the theory of evolution because light is not solid matter and it cannot form solid physical matter.

I realize that this is a profound statement and defies what most people believe or think they know, however, the Bible code could never be solved without first realizing the facts behind what we perceive as solid physical matter as shown through quantum physics.

If you believe God's word is true then I want you to consider something. God's word describes our current reality as temporary and passing away.

The Bible says that real and eternal reality is eternity with the Lord.

If this is true then a spirit being such as an angel, that most people think of as ghost-like because they can pass right through what we think of as our solid physical world, are actually part of the real/eternal reality. The reason they can pass right through our solid physical reality is because our reality is actually just a holographic projection. Man has always viewed it backwards, spirits are not the foggy smoke like less-real reality, we are!

Most people will live their entire lives without ever realizing the facts behind what they perceive as solid physical matter.

What we think of as solid physical matter is actually formed from positive and negative forces in atoms. These forces attract and repel each other to make up all matter in our universe. These forces, simply put, are concentrations of energy.

So why should this matter (no pun intended) to you? It matters because it suggests that the solid physical world you perceive is actually more of an illusion. Einstein realized this.

"Reality is merely an illusion, albeit a very persistent one" -A.Einstein

The study of these subatomic particles and how they interact is called quantum physics.

Niels Henrik David Bohr (7 October 1885 – 18 November 1962) was a Danish physicist who made foundational contributions to understanding atomic structure and quantum theory, for which he received the Nobel Prize in Physics in 1922.

Mr. Bohr had this to say;

"If quantum mechanics hasn't profoundly shocked you, you haven't understood it yet. Everything we call real is made of things that cannot be regarded as real." - Niels Bohr

Quantum physicists discovered that physical atoms are made up of vortices of energy that are constantly spinning and vibrating, each one radiating its own unique energy signature. Therefore, if we really want to observe ourselves and find out what we are, we are beings of energy and vibration, radiating our own unique energy signature -this is fact and is what quantum physics has shown us time and time again.

We are much more than what we perceive ourselves to be, and it's time we begin to see ourselves in that light. If you observed the composition of an atom with a microscope you would see a small, invisible tornado-like vortex, with a number of infinitely small energy vortices called quarks and photons.

These are what make up the structure of the atom. As you focused in closer and closer on the structure of the atom, you would see nothing, you would observe a physical void.

The atom has no physical structure, we have no physical structure, physical things really don't

have any physical structure! Atoms are made out of invisible energy, not tangible matter.

Based on these facts, some of the most brilliant minds have come to the conclusion that these atoms could not have randomly came together to form the order we see in our universe and the world around us.

 The logical conclusion that many have made is that there is a high-tech source code that forms and upholds reality. This theory seems to be supported by codes that have been found in genetic material.

The genetic code is the set of rules by which information encoded within genetic material (DNA or mRNA sequences) is translated into proteins by living cells . ...The code defines how sequences of nucleotide triplets, called codons, specify which amino acid will be added next during protein synthesis.

What would it mean to mankind if there is a more sophisticated code that is behind all matter or reality as we perceive it? It would mean that our reality is similar to a high-tech computer program or, in other words, a digital simulation. This has lead many scientists (physicist) to study and support the holographic principle or the theory that our universe is a very high-tech hologram.

Light does not form solid physical matter but it is the first thing needed in order to form a hologram.

A **hologram** (pronounced HOL-o-gram) is a three-dimensional image, created with photographic projection. The term is taken from the Greek words holos (whole) and gramma (message).

It is not by chance that God's word is His whole message to mankind and His word was the beginning of our reality when He said "Let there be light".

I know the idea of our reality as a hologram by God's design will seem fantastic and maybe even crazy to most people and therefore I will provide amazing evidence for this throughout this book. This evidence will necessarily go over some of the data that I mentioned in former books as well as several new discoveries.

I feel it is necessary to explain this for those who may not have read my other books that include the leg work that leads to what Is one of the most amazing discoveries in human history. For those that have read my other books and will have to endure covering some of the aforementioned data I will say that the bombshell revelation that awaits at the end of this book will make it well worth it and it will only benefit you to review the data that helps connect and confirm the dots that helped lead up to the discoveries made inThe Bible Code Solved.

After all, I am claiming that this code is a primary result of the literal Word of God and that by solving this code you can, and will, literally hear the Voice of God.

Look at this as a type of treasure hunt that puts us on the path that leads to priceless treasure at the end that all reading this get to experience and share.

Proverbs 3:13-15 KJV

13 Happy is the man that findeth wisdom, and the man that getteth understanding.

14 For the merchandise of it is better than the merchandise of silver, and the gain thereof than fine gold.

15 She is more precious than rubies: and all the things thou canst desire are not to be compared unto her.

Proverbs 8:11 KJV

For wisdom is better than rubies; and all the things that may be desired are not to be compared to it.

Proverbs 16:16 KJV

How much better is it to get wisdom than gold!

and to get understanding rather to be chosen than silver!

Job 28:12-24 KJV

12 But where shall wisdom be found? and where is the place of understanding?

13 Man knoweth not the price thereof; neither is it found in the land of the living.

14 The depth saith, It is not in me: and the sea saith, It is not with me.

15 It cannot be gotten for gold, neither shall silver be weighed for the price thereof.

16 It cannot be valued with the gold of Ophir, with the precious onyx, or the sapphire.

17 The gold and the crystal cannot equal it: and the exchange of it shall not be for jewels of fine gold.

18 No mention shall be made of coral, or of pearls: for the price of wisdom is above rubies.

19 The topaz of Ethiopia shall not equal it, neither shall it be valued with pure gold.

20 Whence then cometh wisdom? and where is the place of understanding?

21 *Seeing it is hid from the eyes of all living, and kept close from the fowls of the air.*

22 *Destruction and death say, We have heard the fame thereof with our ears.*

23 God understandeth the way thereof, and he knoweth the place thereof.

24 *For he looketh to the ends of the earth, and seeth under the whole heaven;*

We are given further clues to the location of this treasure we are searching for in those last two verses I listed, 23-24. It literally says that God understands the way and knows the place because He looks to the ends of the earth and sees under the whole heaven.

We will go past the ends of the earth and search the heavens for this clue in the next chapter but for now I want us to get a better understanding of exactly how a hologram is made.

Holograms are made by using a single laser beam. The beam is then split into two beams by a special lens. That way, you get two laser beams that are exactly the same.

 One of those beams is the "reference beam" and is shone directly onto the film.

(The film is basically the same stuff as regular photo film.) The second beam is reflected off of the object that you want to make a hologram of.

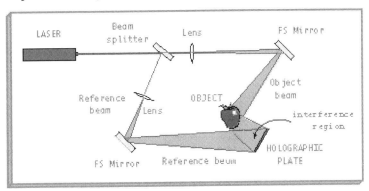

When the two laser beams intersect, they create what's called an interference pattern. This is the pattern that the two sets of waves make when they overlap. (To picture this, you can imagine if you dropped two pebbles into a puddle. The pebbles make waves that go outwards, and when the two sets of waves run into each other, they form a pattern.) That pattern is what's recorded onto the film. Then when the film is developed, you can see the whole image.

Source: https://van.physics.illinois.edu

The beam splitter shown in the photo description above is also known as a partially silvered mirror, or one could say a dim mirror.

If you count the other two mirrors, it takes several reflections even to form a very basic hologram.

1 Corinthians 13:12 NLT

Now we see things imperfectly, like puzzling reflections in a mirror, but then we will see everything with perfect clarity. All that I know now is partial and incomplete, but then I will know everything completely, just as God now knows me completely.

They will see with clarity	יראו בברור
Hidden codes	צפן חבוי
Codes	קדים
In the Torah	בתורה

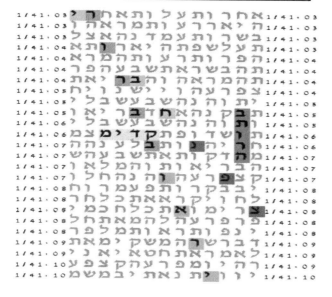

Chapter 3
Searching The Heavens

"The heavens declare the glory of God; and the firmament sheweth his handywork."

-Psalm 19:1 KJV

We have all looked up into the night sky in sheer awe and wonder at the size and beauty of the cosmos. I think this is likely what most people think Psalm 19:1 is saying. What if I told you that it has a deeper meaning and is actually making reference to something much more profound and amazing?

You will understand the full encompassment of Psalm 19:1 by the conclusion of this book but for now I want to point out that the Bible says God is light and in Him there isn't any darkness and yet the universe is over 95% darkness.

John 1:5 KJV

This then is the message which we have heard of him, and declare unto you, that God is light, and in him is no darkness at all.

We must remember that God's whole message to man is His word or the Bible and that the original Greek definition of hologram is literally "whole message".

I have discovered that when I see the word "message" used in the Bible it is usually a clue as to how our holographic reality is formed.

If God is light and the real, eternal, reality with God is also filled with His glory or light, then the default position would actually be light instead of the darkness we see that currently fills our universe. Einstein realized this.

"Darkness does not exist either. Darkness is, in reality, the absence of light. Light we can study, but not darkness. In fact, we can use Newton's prism to break white light into many colors and study the various wavelengths of each color. You cannot measure darkness. A simple ray of light can break into a world of darkness and illuminate it. How can you know how dark a certain space is? You measure the amount of light present. Isn't this correct? Darkness is a term used by man to describe what happens when there is no light present."

So why is our universe over 95% darkness?

Because God placed our universe in a state of darkness as a Judgement against Lucifer.

Isaiah 50:3 KJV

I clothe the heavens with blackness, and I make sackcloth their covering.

To understand the deep prophetic meaning in scripture we need to first realize that most Bible passages that include future prophecies against Israel and other countries also contain a secondary meaning that always points back to Lucifer and his fall.

Ezekiel 28 is a perfect example of this. At first glance, the prophecy in Ezekiel 28:11-19 seems to refer to a human king. The city of Tyre was the recipient of some of the strongest prophetic condemnations in the Bible. However, some of the descriptions in Ezekiel 28:11-19 go beyond any mere human king.

Ezekiel 28:11-19 KJV

11 Moreover the word of the Lord came unto me, saying,

12 Son of man, take up a lamentation upon the king of Tyrus, and say unto him, Thus saith the Lord God; Thou sealest up the sum, full of wisdom, and perfect in beauty.

13 Thou hast been in Eden the garden of God; every precious stone was thy covering, the sardius, topaz, and the diamond, the beryl, the

onyx, and the jasper, the sapphire, the emerald, and the carbuncle, and gold: the workmanship of thy tabrets and of thy pipes was prepared in thee in the day that thou wast created.

14 Thou art the anointed cherub that covereth; and I have set thee so: thou wast upon the holy mountain of God; thou hast walked up and down in the midst of the stones of fire.

15 Thou wast perfect in thy ways from the day that thou wast created, till iniquity was found in thee.

16 By the multitude of thy merchandise they have filled the midst of thee with violence, and thou hast sinned: therefore I will cast thee as profane out of the mountain of God: and I will destroy thee, O covering cherub, from the midst of the stones of fire.

17 Thine heart was lifted up because of thy beauty, thou hast corrupted thy wisdom by reason of thy brightness: I will cast thee to the ground, I will lay thee before kings, that they may behold thee.

18 Thou hast defiled thy sanctuaries by the multitude of thine iniquities, by the iniquity of thy traffick; therefore will I bring forth a fire from the midst of thee, it shall devour thee, and I will bring thee to ashes upon the earth in the sight of all them that behold thee.

19 All they that know thee among the people shall

be astonished at thee: thou shalt be a terror, and never shalt thou be any more.

In no sense could an earthly king claim to be "in Eden" or to be "the anointed cherub who covers" or to be "on the holy mountain of God." Therefore, most Bible interpreters believe that Ezekiel 28:11-19 is a dual prophecy, comparing the pride of the king of Tyre to the pride of Satan.

Another example of this can be found in Jeremiah 4.

Most scholars believe this is a prophecy against Israel but verses 23-28 describe the earth becoming without form and void which ends at 28 by stating that this is the reason that the heavens are black, or in other words the reason for the 95% darkness we have in our universe.

Jeremiah 4:23-28 KJV

23 I beheld the earth, and, lo, it was without form, and void; and the heavens, and they had no light.

24 I beheld the mountains, and, lo, they trembled, and all the hills moved lightly.

25 I beheld, and, lo, there was no man, and all the birds of the heavens were fled.

26 I beheld, and, lo, the fruitful place was a wilderness, and all the cities thereof were broken

down at the presence of the Lord, and by his fierce anger.

27 For thus hath the Lord said, The whole land shall be desolate; yet will I not make a full end.

28 For this shall the earth mourn, and the heavens above be black; because I have spoken it, I have purposed it, and will not repent, neither will I turn back from it.

The first few verses of Isaiah 50 are known as a judgement against the Jews who were sent into Babylon because of their idolatry that broke the covenant, however, Isaiah 50: 2-3 is saying the same exact thing that is mentioned above in Jeremiah 4 verses 25 and 28.

Isaiah 50:2-3 KJV

2 Wherefore, when I came, was there no man? when I called, was there none to answer?

Is my hand shortened at all, that it cannot redeem? or have I no power to deliver? behold, at my rebuke I dry up the sea, I make the rivers a wilderness: their fish stinketh, because there is no water, and dieth for thirst.

***3** I clothe the heavens with blackness, and I make sackcloth their covering.*

In The Matrix Code and The Alien Agenda I gave biblical, scientific, and historical evidence showing that this veil of darkness was God's judgement

against Lucifer for taking on pride and trying to exalt himself to the level of Jesus Christ.

Therefore, I will not go back over those details as my primary focus in this book is to stick with the things that directly involve solving the Bible code.

So what is this veil of darkness? The Bible gives us hints at to what this veil is once we realize that our current reality is holographic. Before we go into these clues I want to point out that holographic does not mean less real.

Our reality is very real to us and as the Bible says we are held responsible for our actions in this reality. We are placed in this reality to make a very important decision that has eternal repercussions. We are here to choose or reject Jesus Christ.

We find a good clue about this veil in Isaiah 50:3.

Isaiah 50:3 KJV

I clothe the heavens with blackness, and I make sackcloth their covering.

Anyone can look up at the night sky and see that there is blackness as the backdrop beyond the stars. If we are to take Isaiah 50:3 literally it would mean that God wrapped the universe with something and this something caused the darkness we see in the universe. So we need to

check the Bible for any other indications as to what exactly God placed over the universe.

The answer is provided in Hebrews 11:3.

Hebrews 11:3 KJV

Through faith we understand that the worlds were framed by the word of God, so that things which are seen were not made of things which do appear.

According to Hebrews 11:3 it's God's word that frames or is wrapped around the universe. This same verse hints that this is also the reason our physical reality is actually holographic as quantum physics suggest.

"so that things which are seen (the physical) are not made of things that do appear" (the non-physical-light, atoms, electrons, neutrons, protons etc).

Our next clue can be found in Jeremiah 4:28

Jeremiah 4:28 KJV

For this shall the earth mourn, and the heavens above be black; because I have spoken it, I have purposed it, and will not repent, neither will I turn back from it.

We see that according to Jeremiah 4:28 whatever causes the heavens to be black also causes the

earth to mourn, or in other words it brings on entropy, decay, and eventual death.

So it causes the universe, and specifically the earth, to go from order and slowly decline into chaos. This seems to go against the theory of evolution that would have us believe that chaos, in the form of the Big Bang, brought order to the universe.

So now you are probably asking yourself; if this wrap that surrounds the universe is the word of God then why would it bring entropy, decay, and eventual death?

We need to understand that Hebrews 11:3 is not referencing the entire word of God, but instead a very specific part of God's word. The part that forms our holographic reality "so that things which are seen are not made of things that do appear."

This confirms what the scribes have been told from the beginning and is also confirmed by several verses in God's word that I will bring up later in this book.

"Even to this day, a Torah scroll is copied by hand from it's predecessor, written out according to unchanging rules, by scribes who undergo an exact detail course of training and preparation. To each of them the following warning has been passed down through the

ages; Should you perchance omit or add one single letter from the Torah, you would thereby destroy all the universe."

ה ו א ו י ה(י)כ א ש ר
כ י ר א ה י(ה)ו ה ב ע
ה ר ע ו ד ל(א)ה ו ת ל
נ א ל ה מ ק(ל)ו ת ו ת
ש ר א ש ר ה(צ)י ל א ל
א א ת ה ת ר(פ)י מ ו י
ח מ ו י ל י(נ)ו ב ה ר
ה ג מ ה ו א(א)ח ר י נ
ו ת ג ש ג מ(ל)א ה ו י
ב נ י ח ש ק(ה)נ פ ש ו
ו א ת ח מ(ד)ר(י)ה מ ו א
ל ו י ס(ע)ו(מ)ב י ת א
ב נ ב(ש)מ ת(א)ש ת ע ש
י מ(נ)י ו י(מ)ת ח ש מ
ל(ר)ע ו ת א(ת)צ א נ א
(מ)ו י ט ב ל ו א ת ה כ

אמת אלהים צפנ אל יה   **Yah is God; God encoded truth.**
Alternate translation: Yah God encoded, God is truth.
נרמ רעש ראה יה   **Yah considered the commotion of their light.**

Chapter 4

Taking a Closer Look At The Torah/Law

"For verily I say unto you, Till heaven and earth pass, one jot or one tittle shall in no wise pass from the law, till all be fulfilled."

-Jesus Christ in **Matthew 5:18 KJV**

It starts to make a lot more sense that God's word would bring entropy to the world when we realize that this is a specific part of God's word, which is the Torah or Law and the Law without Jesus equals death.

Romans 6:23 KJV

For the wages of sin is death; but the gift of God is eternal life through Jesus Christ our Lord.

The Torah/Law is actually a curse to all that do not receive Jesus Christ as their Saviour.

Galatians 3:10-13 KJV

10 For as many as are of the works of the law are under the curse: for it is written, Cursed is every one that continueth not in all things which are written in the book of the law to do them.

11 But that no man is justified by the law in the sight of God, it is evident: for, The just shall live by faith.

12 And the law is not of faith: but, The man that doeth them shall live in them.

13 Christ hath redeemed us from the curse of the law, being made a curse for us: for it is written, Cursed is every one that hangeth on a tree:

When Adam partook of the forbidden fruit he was condemned to death. At this time God removed Adam from of a perfect environment that was in another dimension here on earth, the Garden of Eden, and placed him in an environment that was literally under the Law or veil of darkness that causes the earth to mourn and the heavens above to be black.

This new environment contained entropy which would cause Adam's body to start heading towards decline, or aging, and would eventually lead to his physical death.

We realize that the law brings about death and that this actually caused Adam's death, and yet the Bible says that sin was not held against man until the law was put in place.

There is a great mystery here that we will solve before the conclusion of this book. We have two laws or Torahs which are actually one and the same. One is the source code that forms our holographic reality and is described as a black veil that frames or surrounds our universe. The other is (the same law) the law that Moses received from the Lord written out in 2D.

Both forms of the law create veils and both veils are removed by Jesus Christ.

The 2D version of the law given to Moses represents the veil that was in the temple and torn in two when Jesus paid the price for our sins and hence restoring direct access to Father God for all that receive this free gift. The law that frames our universe also creates the veil of darkness that will be removed by Jesus when He restores the heavens and earth.

If you remember that this veil separates our reality from God's Glory then you will realize that when Jesus removes it He will also be restoring the fullness of the Father's glory to shine upon all creation from that point forward.

We must remember that this veil of darkness is the Law/Torah that was placed over our universe when Lucifer fell.

Therefore, sin started with Lucifer and entered our world from another spiritual dimension when Adam ate the fruit. Something cannot "enter" unless it already exists.

Romans 5:12-14 KJV

12 Wherefore, as by one man sin entered into the world, and death by sin; and so death passed upon all men, for that all have sinned:

13 (For until the law sin was in the world: but sin is not imputed when there is no law.

14 Nevertheless death reigned from Adam to Moses, even over them that had not sinned after the similitude of Adam's transgression, who is the figure of him that was to come.

Verse 13 clearly says that sin is not imputed when there is no law. But we know Adam was sentenced when he ate the fruit. This would not make sense if one did not understand that the veil/Law/Torah was placed over our universe when Lucifer fell and later, when Adam sinned he was kicked out of a perfect environment in another dimension and placed in our current reality that is under the veil of darkness, or Law.

People mistake this for the law of Moses because Moses is mentioned in verse 14. But verse 14 is actually confirming that it isn't the law of Moses by saying that death reigned from Adam to Moses.

The wages of sin is death. Death reigned from Adam to Moses and yet sin is not imputed when there is no law.

For death to reign from Adam to Moses it is making it clear that sin was imputed before Moses and therefore there was a Law in place before Moses was given the 2D Torah.

To further simplify this issue one only need to ask themselves if Adam's partaking of the fruit was considered a transgression and if Adam was punished for this transgression?

Genesis 2:17 KJV

But of the tree of the knowledge of good and evil, thou shalt not eat of it: for in the day that thou eatest thereof thou shalt surely die.

We know Adam ate the fruit, so he definitely committed a transgression and we know the wages of sin is death; "in the day that thou eatest thereof thou shalt surely die." So we know there was an extreme penalty for Adam's sin and that his sin was counted.

I will give a couple more verses that are very hard to rectify if you don't realize that there was a previous earth age and a Law/Torah, or veil of darkness over the universe.

Romans 4:15 ESV

For the law brings wrath, but where there is no law there is no transgression.

Romans 5:13 ESV

for sin indeed was in the world before the law was given, but sin is not counted where there is no law.

Keep in mind that Paul was physically alive when he made the statement in the following verse. Therefore, we can be certain that Paul was making reference to his spirit.

Romans 7:9 KJV

For I was alive without the law once: but when the commandment came, sin revived, and I died.

Jeremiah 4:28 KJV

For this shall the earth mourn, and the heavens above be black; because I have spoken it, I have purposed it, and will not repent, neither will I turn back from it.

This has profound implications when one realizes that sin was not imputed until the law that was put over the universe when Lucifer fell. How do we know there was a previous age that God placed Lucifer in charge of and that some form of humans were there and they actually sinned?

Isaiah 14:12 KJV

How art thou fallen from heaven, O Lucifer, son of the morning! how art thou cut down to the ground, which didst weaken the nations!

We know for a fact Lucifer was already fallen when he tempted Eve in the garden. "which didst (or did, past tense) weaken the nations". At this point it clearly says that Lucifer had already weakened the nations. In other words Lucifer caused the nations to rebel or sin.

This sin was not counted against them because the first age was lit by God's glory. This means the law/Torah/veil of darkness was not put in place yet. Remember, God put this veil/Law in place, that forms our current age and reality, as a judgement against Lucifer when Lucifer tried to exalt himself to the level of God.

We need to realize that amazing biblical info is just surfacing that has previously been overlooked, misunderstood, or taken out of context, during these end times that we currently live in as per Daniel 12:4.

Daniel 12:4 KJV

But thou, O Daniel, shut up the words, and seal the book, even to the time of the end: many shall run to and fro, and knowledge shall be increased.

I give the biblical, scientific, and historical evidence that supports the three ages of the earth in my previous book The Matrix Code and The Alien Agenda.

All the info is there in ways never before understood for anyone who wants to take a look. To explain it in detail in this book would, in my opinion, take us too far off topic as this book is about solving the Bible code.

The fact that the Law/Torah is the veil of darkness, which in turn is the spoken word of God, will be proven by your own ears at the end of this book. We know God did not start creation under the Law or with a judgement. Therefore, the fact that this Law exists and is stretched over our universe proves that creation did not start with our current earth age.

Let's take a closer look at the spoken word of God and see how all this works.

יְ גָדֹאֱלַ יָסְףֱֹבֶַן רְעוֹ אֱֹלֹוֹ צַֹבֶֹ

זֶ הֹנַ יְ דַֹבְֹרֹ יֹהֹנֹה אֱ לֹ מֹשֶֹה וֹ אֱ ל

וְ עֹלַֹ יֹ וֹ שֶֹמֶֹן וְ לֹא יֹתֱֹן עֹלֹ וֹ ל

וְ רֹא יֹ לֹ אֱחֹד כַֹבֹשַֹ אֱחֹד בֹֹן נַֹת

זֹ לֹ אֹמַֹר קֹ חֹ אֱתֹ הֹֹלֹ וֹ יֹ סֹ מֹתֹ דֱֹבָֹ

וֹ לֹ מֹיַֹ אֱ לֹ בֶֹן צֹ וֹ ר יָֹ שֹֹדֹ יֹ וֹ לֹ צַ

אֹתֹ הֹ יֹ כֱמֹתֹ אֱ שֶֹר בֹֹ צַֹ אֹתֹ וֹ רֹ חֹ

אֹתֹ מֹ ן יַֹ דְֹ עֹ וֹ אֱתֹ הֹ אֹרֹ ץ אֱֹ רֹ מֹ

וְ רֹ אֹ לֹ דֹתֹ ן וְ לֹ אֱ בֹ יֹ רֹ סֹ בֹ נַֹ אֱ ל

יֹ בֱֹ נֹ סֹ לֹ כֹ לֹ מֹ ן חֹ תֹ מֹ וֹ לֹ כֹ ל טַֹ א

יֹ בֱֹ נֹ יֹ יֹ שֹ רֹ אֱ לֹ לֹ כֹ ן לֹ אֹתֹ בֹ יֹ א

וֹ גֹ הֹ קֹ עֹ מֹ סֹ הֹ יֹ צֹ אֹ מֹ מֹ צֱֹ רַֹ יֹ סֹ ן יָֹ כֹ

וֹ בֹ לֹ עֹ מֹ סֹ בֱֹ נֹ וֹ בֹ עֹ רֹ וֹ נַֹ אֱ מֹ סֹ הַֹ גֱֹ בֶֹ ר

⬭ Jesus the Messiah

▢ Word of God

Chapter 5

The Spoken Word of God

"Through faith we understand that the worlds were framed by the word of God, so that things which are seen were not made of things which do appear."

-Hebrews 11:3 KJV

I find it very interesting that the Bible clearly says that God spoke our universe into existence, and the Hebrew is one of the the most ancient languages known, and yet when I tell people that the Torah is the source code that forms what we perceive as "Reality" they dismiss it offhand, or worse, accuse me of new age doctrine or practicing Mormonism.

On the most basic level, if God spoke the universe into existence, and He spoke Hebrew, then it makes sense that the Hebrew Torah "The Spoken Word of God" would be the source code beneath all reality.

This is what the Bible clearly says in the plane text.

Hebrews 11:3 KJV

"Through faith we understand that the worlds were framed by the word of God, so that things which are seen were not made of things which do appear."

We can see it says the worlds were framed by the Word of God, but what does it mean by, "things which are seen were not made of things which do appear"?

Quantum physics shows that what we think of as solid matter is actually just positive and negative forces in atoms, therefore everything in our reality that we see is made from things that we cannot see.

But the Bible actually contains the details, on how our reality is generated, in the plain text. The Bible says "The Worlds were "FRAMED" by the Word of God.

Leonard Susskind of the Stanford Institute for Theoretical Physics (who is not a Christian and as far as I know does not even believe in God) Tells how our reality resembles a hologram in his

YouTube video titled "Leonard Susskind on The World As Hologram".

He goes on to say that the advanced math and science indicates that this hologram is generated by a film like layer that contains the information or source code. He concludes by saying that this film surrounds or "FRAMES" our universe and is in the cosmic background.

Leonard came to this conclusion through very advanced mathematical calculations and close studies in quantum physics.

If you are a doubter, and that just seems like a strange coincidence to you, well the "strange coincidences" just keep adding up. If our reality is formed by the Torah, that is a written and very high tech code, then it makes sense, like and computer code, that if you remove any part of the code the program will collapse. in the case of this code it would mean that our reality would cease to exist, or pass away. Is it just coincidence that this is exactly what Jesus said?

Matthew 5:18 (KJV)

18 "For verily I say unto you, Till heaven and earth pass, one jot or one tittle shall in no wise pass from the law, till all be fulfilled."

But what does Jesus mean when He says "Till heaven and earth pass"? The Torah was written on a scroll and it is a black veil or curtain/tent that surrounds our universe. Jesus will roll up this scroll at the end of this age and our current reality will dissolve or cease to exist. This will be when our current heaven and earth will "Pass Away".

Isaiah 34:4 KJV

"And all the host of heaven shall be dissolved, and the heavens shall be rolled together as a scroll: and all their host shall fall down, as the leaf falleth off from the vine, and as a falling fig from the fig tree."

The Torah or veil/curtain that God used to form our reality is actually a curse that God put in place after the fall of Satan. This curse separates our reality from the Light or Glory of God, that is eternity beyond the veil/Torah. Before the fall of Satan, the heavens were lit by Gods Glory and they were beautiful.

JOB 26:11-13

"The pillars of heaven are stunned at His rebuke.

He quiets The sea with his power, and by his understanding He shatters (maw-khats, dashes asunder), Rahab, by His spirit (or Glory) the heavens were BEAUTIFUL; His hand forbids the fugitive snake."

Now our reality is formed by, and under, the Torah/veil of darkness. But when Jesus rolls the heavens/Torah up like a scroll, our reality will once again be lit by God's Glory.

Isaiah 60:19

"The sun shall be no more thy light by day; neither for brightness shall the moon give light unto thee: but the LORD shall be unto thee an everlasting light, and thy God thy glory."

Revelation 21:23

" And the city had no need of the sun, neither of the moon, to shine in it: for the glory of God did lighten it, and the Lamb is the light thereof."

So the first age was lit by the Glory of God and the last age will once again be lit by God's Glory.

2 Corinthians 3:18

"We all, with unveiled faces, are looking as in a

mirror at the glory of the Lord and are being transformed into the same image from glory to

glory; this is from the Lord who is the Spirit."

The Bible mentions this veil in several places. I will give a few examples.

Isaiah 50:3

I clothe the heavens with blackness, and I make sackcloth their covering."

Why Sackcloth?

Smith's Bible Dictionary

Sackcloth

-cloth used in making sacks or bags, a coarse fabric, of a dark color, made of goat's hair-

Sackcloth and ashes were used in Old Testament times as a symbol of debasement, mourning. When someone died, the act of putting on sackcloth showed heartfelt sorrow for the loss of that person.

We see an example of this when David mourned the death of Abner, the commander of Saul's army (2 Samuel 3:31). Jacob also demonstrated his grief by wearing sackcloth when he thought his son, Joseph, has been killed (Genesis 37:34).

These instances of mourning for the dead mention sackcloth but not ashes.

So sackcloth is a fitting description for the veil of darkness God stretched over the universe as He mourned the fall of Satan and the repercussions that followed.

The Bible also calls the veil of darkness a tent that God stretched over the heavens.

Isaiah 40:22

"It is he that sitteth upon the circle of the earth, and the inhabitants thereof are as grasshoppers; that stretcheth out the heavens as a curtain, and spreadeth them out as a tent to dwell in:"

After the fall of Satan God destroyed the former reality and made the earth "without form and void" And he removed His Glory or light at the same time he put the veil of darkness in place. This is why the heavens or universe is black when we look up at the night sky.

Jeremiah 4:23

"I beheld the earth, and, lo, it was without form, and void; and the heavens, and they had no light."

Jeremiah 4:28 KJV

"For this shall the earth mourn, and the heavens above be black: because I have spoken it, I have purposed it, and will not repent, neither will I turn back from it."

So why would the Law or Torah be black and used as a curse? Because the Law or Torah is a curse to all who are not in Christ.

Galatians 3:10 KJV

"For as many as are of the works of the law are under the curse: for it is written, Cursed is every one that continueth not in all things which are written in the book of the law to do them."

Galatians 3:13 KJV

"Christ hath redeemed us from the curse of the law, being made a curse for us: for it is written, Cursed is every one that hangeth on a tree:"

The Sages have been told from the beginning, when copying the Torah, that if they make one mistake they are to burn it because it is the equivalent of destroying the universe.

The universe is a cryptogram set by God Almighty -Isaac Newton

Reality is merely an illusion, albeit a very persistent one -A. Einstein.

"If quantum mechanics hasn't profoundly shocked you, you haven't understood it yet. Everything we call real is made of things that cannot be regarded as real." - Niels Bohr.

Bible Code(539) Exists in the human langage(-539)																				539 (1)
א	ר	י	ת	ן	ע	מ	ל	ת	ת	ש	ר	ל	ת	מ	ש	ס	י	ר	ב	5: 6: 1
י	צ	ו	ה	ר	ש	א	ה	ו	ה	י	ת	א	ה	כ	ש	ת	ן	פ	ד	5: 6: 12
ת	ב	א	ל	ע	ב	ש	נ	ר	ש	א	ץ	ר	א	ה	ת	א	ו	נ	ל	5: 6: 23
ו	מ	א	ל	ה	מ	ד	א	ה	י	נ	פ	ל	ע	ר	ש	א	ס	י	מ	5: 7: 6
ן	י	ל	ח	ל	כ	ד	מ	מ	ה	ו	ה	י	ו	י	ס	נ	ה	ד	ת	5: 7: 14
י	מ	ש	ה	ת	ה	ת	מ	ס	מ	ש	ת	א	ת	ד	ב	א	ה	ו	ד	5: 7: 24
ל	ו	נ	י	כ	ר	ד	ב	ת	כ	ל	ל	ד	י	ה	ל	א	ה	ו	ה	5: 8: 6
ד	י	ס	צ	ע	ו	י	ח	כ	ד	ב	ב	ל	ב	ת	ר	מ	א	ו	ד	5: 8: 16
צ	ב	א	ל	ד	י	נ	פ	מ	ס	ש	י	ו	ו	מ	ה	ו	ה	י	ת	5: 9: 4
ל	ס	י	נ	ב	א	ה	ת	ח	ל	י	נ	ש	ת	א	י	ל	א	ה	ו	5: 9: 11
ע	ב	ס	ג	ל	ל	פ	ת	א	ו	ו	ד	י	מ	ש	ה	ל	ד	א	מ	5: 9: 20
ב	ס	ת	מ	ה	ל	ס	א	י	צ	ו	ה	ס	ת	ו	א	ו	ת	א	נ	5: 9: 28
ל	ו	כ	ל	ע	ה	ז	ה	ס	ו	י	ה	ד	ע	ו	מ	ש	ב	ד	ר	5: 10: 8
ח	ק	י	א	ל	ו	ס	י	נ	פ	א	ש	י	א	ל	ר	ש	א	א	ו	5: 10: 17
נ	ב	ס	ר	י	ב	א	ל	ו	ו	ת	ד	ל	ה	ש	ע	ר	ש	א	ו	5: 11: 6
כ	צ	ר	א	ר	ט	מ	י	ת	ה	נ	ו	ס	כ	ש	פ	נ	ל	כ	ב	5: 11: 13
ס	י	ו	ג	ס	ת	ש	ר	י	ו	ס	כ	י	נ	פ	ל	מ	ה	ל	א	5: 11: 23
ש	י	ו	ה	ת	א	ס	ת	ש	ר	י	ו	ס	כ	ל	ן	ת	נ	ס	כ	5: 11: 31
ע	ת	א	ל	ד	י	ה	ל	א	ה	ו	ה	י	ד	כ	ר	ב	ר	ש	א	5: 12: 7
ה	ק	ר	ל	י	א	כ	ו	י	ב	צ	כ	ו	נ	ל	כ	א	י	ר	ו	5: 12: 15

Bible Code (539) Exists in the human langauge (-539)

Chapter 6

Evidence That Our Universe Could Be A Digital Simulation/Hologram

"This unsuspected connection suggests that these codes may be ubiquitous in nature, and could even be embedded in the essence of reality. If this is the case, we might have something in common with the Matrix science-fiction films, which depict a world where everything human being's experience is the product of a virtual-reality-generating computer network."

-Theoretical physicist, Dr. James Gates, Jr.

It is hard to argue that the Bible code itself is the program code that forms our holographic reality if one is still questioning the authenticity of the code. Hopefully we can put that to rest before we continue any further.

Ordinarily we would assume that the US Pentagon and anything having to do with the Bible would be far removed from one another.

 But in 1994 statistical science, a respected mathematical Journal, published report number

three, volume 9 titled-

"Equal distant letter sequences in the book of Genesis."

 That report found its way to the Pentagon's national secret agency of cryptology. And made it to the desk of Harold Gans, a senior cryptographer for the Pentagon's national security agency. Gans knew that equal letter Skip sequence was a code form widely used by governments and their agents.

The idea that they would occur in the book of Genesis was hard for him to believe. He found it so difficult to believe that he wrote his own computer program based on his intimate knowledge of encryption techniques with the intent of disproving the results published by Statistical Science.

 If the codes were simply a matter random chance then Gan's program would reveal this. After testing the codes with this program Gans made the statement "The probability that these codes could appear by accident is virtually non-existent!"

The late Michael Talbot published the book The Holographic Universe in 1991.

Michael had this to say;

"Put it another way, there is evidence to suggest that our world and everything in it- from snowflakes to maple trees to falling stars and spinning electrons-are also only ghostly images, projections from a level of reality so beyond our own it is literally beyond both space and time."

Jim Elvidge has worked with cutting-edge digital technology for decades. He holds a masters degree in electrical engineering from Cornell University as well as multiple patents in digital signal processing, and he has published papers about remote sensing and other related topics in peer-reviewed journals.

Combining his knowledge of digital systems with quantum mechanics, Elvidge has found that we may be living in something like a computer program. The matter, the "stuff" we seem to touch and feel, is actually, mostly, empty space. Our senses deceive us.

Our world isn't necessarily a computer program designed by parasitic futuristic robots like in the movie "The Matrix." But it does bear a striking resemblance to a digital simulation or computer program, according to engineer Jim Elvidge.

Eliyahu Rips, born 12 December 1948, is an Israeli mathematician of Latvian origin known for his research in geometric group theory.

He became known to the general public following his co-authoring a paper on what is popularly known as Bible code, the supposed coded messaging in the Hebrew text of the Torah.

Mr. Rips has this to say;

"It may be some form of information we cannot yet fully imagine, something that would be as strange to us now as a computer would have been to people 3,000 years ago.

"It is almost certainly many more levels deep, but we do not have a powerful enough mathematical model to reach it," says Rips. "It is probably less like a crossword puzzle and more like a HOLOGRAM.

"We are looking at two-dimensional arrays and we probably should look in at least three dimensions, but we don't know how." No one can explain how the code was created.

Every scientist, every mathematician, and physicist who understands the code, agree that not even the fastest supercomputers we have today - not even all of the computers now in the world working together - could have encoded the Bible in the way it was done 3,000 years ago. "I can't even imagine how it would be done, how anyone could have done it," says Rips. "It is a mind beyond our imagination."

"In the end", says Rips, "the amount of information is incalculable and probably infinite. And that is only the first, crudest level of The Bible (mathematical) code."

What Mr. Rips means by this being the crudest level of the Bible code is the fact that they are studying the 2D version as it is laid out in the Torah. He can see that it goes holographic but they don't know how to access it.

By solving this code one should have the keys to access the holographic information contained in the deeper levels of the Bible code. However, this key will still need to be combined with a computer that can process mass amounts of data as the holographic Torah will contain all information in the universe from the beginning to the end of time.

Even when they key is revealed it is still doubtful that even the most powerful quantum computers could process the information. Only time will tell.

This will probably be the best evidence proving the existence of God that has ever been revealed and this testimony to the existence of God is what keeps me moving forward to reveal this information to as many as are willing to read this book and hear it for themselves. However, I would be lying if I said that I wasn't also concerned with what this info could do if it falls into the wrong hands.

Anyone can hear and hence verify that this is real, but only someone with access to a quantum computer would have any chance at processing this massive amount of data, if indeed it can be processed.

Despite how extreme the idea sounds, theories about the Universe being an illusion or a hologram aren't new. Now, researchers claim to have found evidence towards proving this hypothesis.

A team of theoretical physicists at the University of Southampton believes it has found signs our Universe is an illusion by studying the cosmic microwave background (CMB) – radiation left over from the Big Bang.

A holographic Universe means information that makes up what we perceive as a 3D reality is stored on a 2D surface, including time. This means, essentially, everything you see and experience is an illusion.

"Imagine that everything you see, feel and hear in three dimensions, and your perception of time, in fact emanates from a flat two-dimensional field," says Professor Kostas Skenderis from the University of Southampton.

While theories of holographic universes have

been around since the 1990s, the latest study, published in the journal Physical Review Letters, contains the first proof, the researchers say.

"We are proposing using this holographic Universe, which is a very different model of the Big Bang than the popularly accepted one that relies on gravity and inflation,"

said Niayesh Afshordi, from the University of Waterloo and Perimeter Institute, and lead author of the study.

"Each of these models makes distinct predictions that we can test as we refine our data and improve our theoretical understanding, all within the next five years," Afshordi said. "Holography is a huge leap forward in the way we think about the structure and creation of the Universe," added Skenderis.

Source: http://www.wired.co.uk/article/our-universe-is-a-hologram

Similarly, in 1982 a landmark experiment performed by a research team led by physicist Alain Aspect at the Institute of Theoretical and Applied Optics, in Paris, demonstrated that the web of subatomic particles that compose our physical universe-the very fabric of reality itself-possesses what appears to be an undeniable "holographic" property.

Theoretical physicist, Dr. James Gates, Jr. discovered binary code at the quantum level. We are talking about quantum bits of 1's and 0's.

The idea that we live in a holographic universe that uses a form of quantum "computer code" to create the physical reality is not a new idea. In the 1940s, some physicists suggested that we live in a "computer generated" universe. Physicists James Gates talks about this form of computer code, which he refers to as "adinkras" in the YouTube video titled "Theoretical Physicist Finds Computer Code in String Theory".

The core structures of reality work similar to how a computer works. A computer communicates and operates through the use of binary codes, which are codes that consist of ones (on) and zeros (off). Binary codes are very simple but with the right combinations they can help computers create magnificent things.

For example, when we paint a picture using a computer software, the core state of the colors and shapes in the picture are basically made of ones and zeros.

We do not see our picture as ones and zeros, because the central processing unit (CPU) and its counterparts process the binary codes as colors and shapes. The greatest thing about binary codes is that there are no limits to their combinations.

The simple process of using binary codes to create things within the hardware of computers is very similar to how Creation creates our external reality or material world. The material world works very similar to a virtual reality. At its core, the material world is made of only light (energy) that flashes on and off to create energy codes.

The idea that we live in a holographic universe is very real. With the invention of quantum computers, physicists should soon be able to prove this beyond a reasonable doubt.

So, what does it mean that we live in a holographic universe generated by some kind of quantum computer? It means that the Universe was created by an intelligent creator, and therefore it was not created by accident. In other words, the Prime Creator exists!

Source: **https://www.sott.net/article/301611-Living-in-the-Matrix-Physicist-finds-computer-code-embedded-in-string-theory**

"Reality is merely an illusion, albeit a very persistent one"

-Albert Einstein

○ EINSTEIN ⬠ THEY PROPHESIED A BRAINY PERSON

◇ SCIENCE ▢ A NEW AND EXCELLENT UNDERSTANDING

△ HE OVERTURNED PRESENT REALITY

Chapter 7
Searching The Universe For The
Source of The Hologram

"The universe is like a safe to which there is a combination. But the combination is locked up in the safe."

-Peter De Vries

The truth always brings loose ends together, makes more sense out of theories, and fits the overall picture. This would explain why quantum physics shows our universe resembling a hologram.

 It would also explain why the Big Bang theory has been the best attempt, so far, to explain the origins of our universe. The projected hologram would resemble a Big Bang as the universe's beginning would be a projection of concentrated light which would then expand out from its point of origin.

So this begs the question, is there anything we can observe in the universe that would be the equivalent of an enormous projection of light?

We have all heard of a black hole which seems to be the exact opposite of what we are looking for here. In theory, a black hole takes in all information and distributes it along the surface. What we are looking for would be something that projects outwards (the Glory of God) that would resemble a vortex of light. So in a sense what we're looking for has all the attributes of the theoretical white hole.

The following is an excerpt from **http://nautil.us/blog/white-holes-could-existbut-thatdoesnt-mean-they-do**

Black holes are common in the cosmos-nearly every large galaxy harbours a super-massive one in its nucleus, not to mention smaller specimens.

However, astronomers have yet to identify a single white hole. That doesn't rule out their existence entirely since it might be hard to see one: if they effectively repel particles, there is a small possibility they could be lurking out there somewhere, invisible. Nevertheless, none of all the diverse objects astronomers have observed seem to resemble what we'd expect from white holes.

The Big Bang actually works like a white hole in many respects, and maybe the closest our universe ever gets to having one.

It lies in the past for any observer in the universe, and all we see expanded outward from it. However, it didn't have an event horizon (meaning it was something called a "naked singularity", which is far less kinky than it sounds). Despite that, it resembles gravitational collapse in reverse.

So where do we even start, when given the great expanse of the universe, to look for this white hole? I believe the Bible gives us clues as to where to start our search. The Bible indicates that man and the Earth we live on are the apex or center of God's creation and modern science confirms this.

The Modern World is Faced with the Breach of a Far Reaching Paradigm.

Most cosmologists will not admit it publicly, but perhaps over a beer, they would tell you what is happening. Observations over the last 50 years, culminating with the Planck satellite results (March 2013) set modern science on a counter-revolution leading closer to ideas formed 500 years ago.

Today's cosmology is based on two broad principles: The Copernican Principle (we are not in a special place in the universe) and the Cosmological Principle (The Copernican Principle, plus isotropy- the view from anywhere in the universe looks about the same).

 Starting with early studies of the cosmic microwave background (CMB), and in recent years culminating with results from the COBE then the WMAP satellites, scientists were faced with a signal at the largest scales of the universe- a signal that pointed right back at us, indicating that we are in a special place in the universe. Without getting overly technical, the Copernican and cosmological principles require that any variation in the radiation from the CMB be more or less randomly distributed throughout the universe, especially on large scales.

Results from the WMAP satellite (the early 2000s) indicated that when looking at large scales of the universe, the noise could be partitioned into "hot" and "cold" sections and this partitioning is aligned with our ecliptic plane and equinoxes. This partitioning and alignment resulted in an axis through the universe, which scientists dubbed "the axis of evil", because of the damage it does to their theories.

 This axis is aligned to us. Lawrence Krauss commented in 2005:

" But when you look at [the cosmic microwave background] map, you also see that the structure that is observed, is in fact, in a weird way, correlated with the plane of the earth around the sun. Is this Copernicus coming back to haunt us? That's crazy. We're looking out at the whole universe.

There's no way there should be a correlation of structure with our motion of the earth around the sun—the plane of the earth around the sun—the ecliptic. That would say we are truly the center of the universe."

Most scientists brushed the observation off as a fluke of some type, and many theories were created to explain it away. Many awaited the Planck mission.

The Planck satellite was looked upon as a referee for these unexpected (and unwelcome) results. The Planck satellite used different sensor technology, and an improved scanning pattern to map the CMB.

In March 2013, Planck reported back, and in fact verified the presence of the signal in even higher definition than before!

There are cosmologists and scientists who recognise the signal for what it is, and recent articles have started talking about the need for some "new physics" to explain the results.

Even on the Planck mission website, Professor Efstathiou states: "Our ultimate goal would be to construct a new model that predicts the anomalies and links them together.

But these are early days; so far, we don't know whether this is possible and what type of new physics might be needed. And that's exciting"

Other observations have independently validated the "axis of evil" in recent years, and this adds credibility to the CMB observations. These observations include galaxy rotation alignments to our tiny part of the universe.

Very recent reports include observations of alignment between "sky distributions of powerful extended quasars and some other sub-classes of radio galaxies" and "a plane passing through the two equinoxes and the north celestial pole (NCP)".

Also, anisotropy of cosmic acceleration in Union2 Type Ia supernova appear to be aligning with the CMB features.

All this supports the contention that the Copernican Principle (and cosmological) have effectively been invalidated without even discussing the quantisation of various astronomical features about us, which further support the contention.

The question is 'what will modern science do now?

Will they invent additional parameters to keep the current theories alive (in addition to those already added: dark matter, dark energy, red-shift as expansion, big bang inflation, etc.) or will they consider the possibility that we are in a special place as observations clearly indicate?

Source: https://medium.com/we-are-in-a-specialplace/planck-satellite-confirms-wmap-findings-universeis-not-copernican-

If we are truly at the center of the universe, as the evidence clearly indicates, and the universe starts at the point of creation and then expands out from there, it would make sense that the source of the hologram should be somewhere in our own neighbourhood. But do we have any evidence that this is the case?

The following is an excerpt from http://physics.stackexchange.com/questions/2073 17/coul d-the-black-hole-in-the-center-of-the-galaxy-be-a-whitehole

Could the black hole in the center of the galaxy be a white hole?

In the center of the galaxy, there is a strong radio source which we call Sagittarius A*.

Based on the high speed and orbit of nearby stars we have calculated that something with the mass of more than 4 million Sun's is located in this small area of space.

And such a big mass in such a small area can only be a black hole, and the observed electromagnetic radiation comes from the accretion disk of the black hole. But there is also another solution to this method of logic deduction, Sagittarius A* might optionally be a white hole.

Like black holes, white holes have properties like mass, charge, and angular momentum. They attract matter like any other mass, but objects falling towards a white hole would never actually reach the white hole's event horizon. And if we look at the observations this solution seems to fit beautifully:

Sagittarius A* don't have any "appetite". The Chandra telescope observes a lot of gas close to Sag A*, and this gas is ejected outwards by an unknown mechanism.

We have never observed anything going into Sag A*, but based on the light given off by Sag A* the researchers have calculated that less than 1 % is "eaten" by the black hole and more than 99 % is the ejected gas we observe.

The gas is not ejected outwards by gravitational slingshot effects, as it is too close and has too little velocity, tidal forces ejecting material is one hypothesis they are working on to explain this mystery. If Sag A* is a black hole it seems like there is some strange physics going on, if Sag A* is a white hole, ejection of material is what we would expect.

Light is flowing from a much larger area than a tiny accretion disk of a black hole. If energy, matter, and antimatter is pouring in through Sag A* this will create light.

The Chandra telescope did neither observe the accretion disk which we expected to see with

Chandra's high detail and resolution, only gas being ejected from Sag A*.

A large area around Sag A* is energised. A black hole doesn't energise nearby space much but mostly energises a tiny accretion disk. Close to the galactic center we observe the formation of many new stars, it is the most massive breeding ground for new stars in the galaxy and a large area close to the galactic center is populated by young stars.

A black hole would devour stars instead of giving birth to stars, while a white hole would give excellent conditions for star birth.

Neither have we observed any star being devoured by Sag A*, or anything else, and we have observed it for 40 years. In 2011 the scientists got excited, a huge cloud of gas called G2 was accelerating towards Sagittarius A*, they expected that the black hole to pull apart and devour the gas cloud and the accretion disk of the black hole would light up.

But it was a big flop as the accretion disk showed no sign of lighting up and nothing extra was eaten, and it is a mystery that G2 was not ripped apart by the strong gravitational forces of the black hole. Now they speculate if G2 actually is a star.

Well if it is a star, and it is not feeding the black hole, could it instead feed itself? We observe a large cloud of antimatter in the galactic center,

where the highest intensity of the signature frequency is at Sag A*.

If there is antimatter flowing in from the white hole, creation of antimatter by acceleration effects or pure energy that creates antimatter and matter in a process similar to the Big Bang this would explain the antimatter.

Today the antimatter is explained by being created by some binary X-ray stars close to the galactic center, but why do we then only see this behaviour for these binary stars and not all the millions of others?

They neither know how these stars potentially produce the antimatter or why the amount is so high.

The universe is expanding at an accelerated speed. This requires energy to be added, and if energy pours in through white holes, energy is added.

We have never observed any singularity, so why should a black hole singularity exist? Information seems to be lost in a black hole singularity, which goes against the rules of quantum mechanics; a white hole would be a solution to this black hole information paradox.

Two gigantic fermi bubbles extend up and down from the galactic center, for at least 30,000 light years.

These bubbles require vast amounts of energy to be created and can't be created by a slumbering black hole accretion disk. So the scientist suggests that the black hole had an eruption 2 million years ago.

Instead of erupting black holes, a white hole could fuel the fermi bubbles. If we just look at these observations it might seem like they count in favor of Sag A* being a white hole.

And it is an important question, as science is currently stuck with the option that Sag A* is a black hole singularity. If there is a white hole in the center of the galaxy instead, the implications are enormous and it could give us answers to many grand problems in astrophysics.

Is it just coincidence that the only strong evidence we have in the entire universe for a white hole just happened to be in our neighbourhood? I don't believe so.

In Torah(-3916) skip(3916) computer(3915) secret(-3916)	-3916 (1)
א ו ס י ע י ה ת א ו ה ר י ס ה ת א ה ב ז	2: 38: 3
ד ע ו מ ל ה א ו י ב ר י כ ה ת א ת ה נ ו	2: 40: 7
ת א ו ב ר ק ה ל ע ו ש א ב ל ח ה ל כ ת א	3: 3: 14
ה ל ע ש א ה ו ו ו ה ט ס ו ק מ ל א ה נ ח	3: 6: 4
ה י ד י ת א ו י נ ב ו ו ו ה א ו כ מ ס י	3: 8: 22
נ ל כ מ ו ס י מ ה צ ו ש ל כ מ ס י ל ח נ	3: 11: 10
י א ל ק ת נ ה ת א ו ה ל ג ת ה ו ו ו ע ה	3: 13: 32
ת י ב ב א ו ה ת ו א מ מ ת ע ו צ ת י ב ב	3: 14: 44
ו ס י מ ב ו ו ש ב ת א צ ה ו ו ו י ד ג ב	3: 16: 28
א ו י ת י ש ד ק מ ו ו ו מ ש ה י ת ת ב ש	3: 19: 30
ס ה י ו ד נ ל כ ל ו נ ב ו ק א י ו ק י ו	3: 22: 18
ו ב ש ו ל ה ש ע י ו כ ה ש ע ו ש א כ ו ת	3: 24: 19
א ת א ל ו י ו ק י מ ע ו כ ל ה ס א ו ו י	3: 26: 20
כ ס ת ל ג ל ג ל ת ו מ ש ו פ ס מ ב ו י ד	4: 1: 22
ו ל ה ת ח פ ש מ ס ה ה ל א י ש ו מ ו י ל	4: 3: 20
ה ש מ ד ק פ ו ש א ס י ד ק פ ה ל כ ה ש מ	4: 4: 45
ה ל ק ש מ ה א מ ו ס י ש ל ש ה ת א ף ס כ	4: 7: 13
פ ו כ נ ס י ו ל ה ת א ו ו ה ת א ף י כ ה ו	4: 8: 11
ו ה ה ס ו ק מ ה ס ו ש א ר ק י ו ש א ה ע ק	4: 11: 2
ה ת א ו נ ש ו י ו ה ל ע נ ה ל ע ו מ א י	4: 13: 30

In Torah(-3916) skip(3916) computer(3915) secret(-3916)

Chapter 8

Quantum Entanglement, The Omnipresence Of God

"THE DAY SCIENCE BEGINS TO STUDY NON-PHYSICAL PHENOMENA, IT WILL MAKE MORE PROGRESS IN ONE DECADE THAN IN ALL THE PREVIOUS CENTURIES OF ITS EXISTENCE."

— Nikola Tesla

When one realizes that reality is similar to a high-tech digital simulation or computer program, then one can come to terms with the fact that nothing that happens within this reality is by chance or accident. What's more, one also realizes that God is aware of even the finest details as they are all part of the program that He designed.

Not only did God design this program but it works by His power and literally through Him. This means God is actually part of the program, the central critical foundation of the program, or the pyramid shaped quantum tetrahedron that represents Jesus Christ.

This explains why God has complete and total awareness of what occurs within our reality.

If a single grain of sand breaks free because of a slight breeze and tumbles a few feet on a beach God is aware.

This is why the Bible says that even the number of hairs on your head are accounted for. With some aging men this may not appear as fantastic as it actually is, as they too can likely tell you the number of hairs on their head.

Joking aside, this is amazing info that helps us understand our holographic reality.

Luke 12:6-7 KJV

6 *Are not five sparrows sold for two farthings, and not one of them is forgotten before God?*

7 *But even the very hairs of your head are all numbered. Fear not therefore: ye are of more value than many sparrows.*

If reality is holographic it would mean that everything in the universe is actually connected. Since we are within the code, vast distances and the physical are real to us, however, at the quantum level even vast distance would be meaningless as it is all connected and therefore instantly accessible.

At the quantum level particles react instantly even when separated by vast distances.

If this concept seems a little far-fetched to you I want you to consider what is known as quantum entanglement.

According to Wikipedia quantum entanglement is a physical phenomenon that occurs when pairs or groups of particles are generated or interact in ways such that the quantum state of each particle cannot be described independently of the others, even when the particles are separated by a large distance—instead, a quantum state must be described for the system as a whole.

Measurements of physical properties such as position, momentum, spin, and polarization, performed on entangled particles are found to be appropriately correlated. For example, if a pair of particles are generated in such a way that their total spin is known to be zero, and one particle is found to have clockwise spin on a certain axis, the spin of the other particle, measured on the same axis, will be found to be counterclockwise, as to be expected due to their entanglement.

However, this behavior gives rise to paradoxical effects: any measurement of a property of a particle can be seen as acting on that particle (e.g., by collapsing a number of superposed states) and will change the original quantum property by some unknown amount; and in the case of entangled particles, such a measurement will be on the entangled system as a whole.

It thus appears that one particle of an entangled pair "knows" what measurement has been performed on the other, and with what outcome, even though there is no known means for such information to be communicated between the particles, which at the time of measurement may be separated by arbitrarily large distances.

This is why all correct findings in real science will always point to Jesus and confirm God's word. Let me give a few examples of this.

In vortex math there is a pattern that repeats itself. This pattern is 1,2, and 4 on one side, and 5, 7, and 8, on the other. This pattern is the grid that forms the energy that we pay for in the form of electricity. If you look at the grid you will notice that 3, 6, and 9 are outside of this pattern. This means 3, 6, and 9 do not have any resistance or in other words 3, 6, and 9 equal free energy.

Nikola Telsa knew this.

"If you knew the magnificence of the three, six and nine, you would have a key to the universe."
– Nikola Tesla

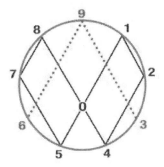

This is why the power and money loving Elitist suppressed Telsa's discovery of free energy.

Remember 3,6, and 9 represent free energy, or one could say freedom. If you connect the 3, 6, and 9 you will get a pyramid. As we went over earlier the pyramid represents Jesus Christ as the head stone.

John 8:36 KJV

If the Son therefore shall make you free, ye shall be free indeed.

We can take this further and equate the free energy generated by 3, 6, and 9, that form the pyramid shape, with Jesus Christ who offers us the only truly free gift that can save us.

"Salvation is only found in Jesus"

Acts 4:12 KJV

Neither is there salvation in any other: for there is none other name under heaven given among men, whereby we must be saved.

One final note: The VBM people (Vortex Based Math) people believe that this diagram is a "divine code," but whether or not you believe Galileo's statement "Mathematics is the language with which God has written the universe," there is no denying that base ten is an entirely human construction.

There are other things that we perceive in our reality that I do not believe are by chance.

The Bible says God is light.

1 John 1:5 KJV

This then is the message which we have heard of him, and declare unto you, that God is light, and in him is no darkness at all.

God/Jesus Christ are also described as "Living Water".

Jeremiah 2:13 KJV

13 For my people have committed two evils; they have forsaken me the fountain of living waters, and hewed them out cisterns, broken cisterns, that can hold no water.

Jeremiah 17:13 KJV

13 O Lord, the hope of Israel, all that forsake thee shall be ashamed, and they that depart from me shall be written in the earth, because they have forsaken the Lord, the fountain of living waters.

The appearance of the Glory of the Lord is said to be surrounded by a rainbow.

Ezekial 1:28 NASB

As the appearance of the rainbow in the clouds on a rainy day, so was the appearance of the surrounding radiance. Such was the appearance of the likeness of the glory of the LORD. And when I saw it, I fell on my face and heard a voice speaking.

If we recall God's promise to Noah it was to remember when we see a rainbow that He will never flood the earth again. Now you know why He used a rainbow.

Genesis 9:11-13 KJV

11 And I will establish my covenant with you, neither shall all flesh be cut off any more by the waters of a flood; neither shall there any more be a flood to destroy the earth.

12 *And God said, This is the token of the covenant which I make between me and you and every living creature that is with you, for perpetual generations:*

13 *I do set my bow in the cloud, and it shall be for a token of a covenant between me and the earth.*

Now remember that God is light and Jesus Christ is Living Water. When the light shines through the water we get a rainbow which is God's promise to man to never destroy the world by flood again.

Do you think this is all just coincidence?

As you read on you will see that the coincidences just keep adding up.

The Bible says that God spoke our universe into existence. We know that the sounds of our voice are caused by the vibrations in our vocal cords. Sound is vibration and all physical matter is just energy vibrating at different frequencies.

 "If you want to find the secrets of the universe, think in terms of energy, frequency and vibration." -Nikola Tesla

According to modern science the universe formed faster than the speed of light and yet we know light travels faster than anything in existence. So how is that possible?

They will tell you that this is due to cosmic inflation. However, this is just their way of inventing an explanation for something that they have absolutely no idea about. Without the word of God as a guidline, since God is the Creator, all they can do is speculate.

Yes, they do invent totally fabricated ideas with absolutely no bases in reality to explain things they don't understand.

Dark matter is one example of this and the multi-universe is another very good example.

So why did they invent the multi-universe hypothesis? Simply put, it is because our universe is a holographic reality that leaves no room for error.

What do I mean by that?

Leonard Susskind, theoretical physics at Stanford University, in a YouTube interview titled "Leonard Susskind - Is the Universe Fine-Tuned for Life and Mind?" had this to say;

"Everything seems to be almost on a knife's edge. If your were to change the laws of physics even a little bit the world as we know it wouldn't exist."

The host goes on to ask Leonard; "How many of these constants or laws of physics would fit into this category of fine tuning?" The host then says, "Lets talk about one in particular, the cosmological constant".

Leonards response was; "That's the one that is really on a knife's edge.

It is on such a narrow knife edge that it is almost inconceivable, if you were to change it just the tiniest, tiniest bit we could not be here." How tiny you ask yourself? Leonard says it is one part in a zillion, zillion, zillion etc. eventually equalling one-hundred and twenty-three zeros to one. It's beyond any mathematical possibility of chance.

Why is it beyond any possibility of chance? Because when you exist in a holographic program nothing happens by chance.

 For example, it is not by chance that the original Greek definition of Hologram is "Whole Message" and God's Word is His whole message to mankind and God's Word, The Torah/Law, is literally what forms our holographic reality.

Modern science can only hypothesize about reality being similar to a holographic projection.

But, as Christians that believe the word of God is one-hundred percent truth, we don't need to hypothesize about the make-up of our reality because the Bible tells us exactly how reality is formed down to the finest detail and real science will always confirm God's Word.

For example, you can take a holographic plate (the film or plastic card that a holographic image is stored on) let's say it's a hologram of a bird that is on the plate, and you can cut it into pieces.

After you have cut it into pieces you will find that each piece still contains the complete image, the bird in this example, that forms the hologram.

Now let's apply this holographic fact to our own reality based on real science and God's word.

Our reality is made in the image of God/Jesus Christ who represents the pyramid shape. If you were to cut our reality into the finest pieces that make it up, the Planck Length formed pyramid, each piece would still contain the complete image of our reality which is Jesus Christ or the quantum level pyramid shape.

This could explain how God is omnipresent in our universe.

This does not mean that Jesus isn't also God in the flesh who came to our fallen holographic reality as a man and paid the price for our sins.

Like I said, holographic does not mean less real. Our reality is very real to us and we are accountable for everything we do in our reality. Jesus knew this and He also knew that He was our only chance at redemption.

Genesis 1:27 KJV

So God created man in his own image, in the image of God created he him; male and female created he them.

We find the image of Jesus Christ in the smallest division that forms our reality which brings us back to Colossians 1:16-18.

Colossians 1:16-18 KJV

16 *For by him were all things created, that are in heaven, and that are in earth, visible and invisible, whether they be thrones, or dominions, or principalities, or powers: all things were created by him, and for him:*

17 *And he is before all things, and by him all things consist.*

18 And he is the head of the body, the church: who is the beginning, the firstborn from the dead; that in all things he might have the preeminence.

It is not by chance that every detail of verses 16-18 line up with the position, shape, and function

of the pyramid shape and light at the quantum level.

John 1:4 KJV

In him was life; and the life was the light of men.

So how is it possible that every detail of the universe we exist in can be found in the Bible that is at least 2,000 years old even in the New Testament text?

It is because the spoken Word of God truly is the source code that forms our reality. This is the reason that they can find codes in the 2D version of the Torah that contain the details of what goes on in our reality.

This is also the reason the Bible suggest two different versions of the same Torah. The one that was taken down by Moses directly from the mouth of God and the one that God actually used to speak our reality into existence.

If we could locate this first Torah, that is the actual words God used to speak our reality into existence, what would it look like? What type of matter would it be made out of, if any, and how exactly would it work?

All those questions and more will be answered with biblical and scientific evidence in the remainder of this book.

The Messiah, Jesus Christ, is literally the light that forms our reality!

John1:1-4 KJV

1In the beginning was the Word (Jesus Christ), and the Word was with God, and the Word was God.

2 The same was in the beginning with God.

3 All things were made by him; and without him was not any thing made that was made.

4 In him was life; and the life was the LIGHT of men.

Messiah	משיח	Passover	פסח
5768	התשסח	Holiday of Matzah	בחג המצות
Repentance	תשובה	Holiday of Sukkot	בחג הסכות
Luria	לוריא	Gog	גוג
Light 45 52	אר מה בן		

Chapter 9

Searching For The Physical Matter That Contains The Holographic Information

"It is almost certainly many more levels deep, but we do not have a powerful enough mathematical model to reach it. It is probably less like a crossword puzzle and more like a hologram."

-Eliyahu Rips commenting on the Bible Codes

Using the Bible as our map and modern science to verify and confirm our findings we will go on a quest in search for the mysterious substance that forms the veil that God placed over the universe.

We know eternity is lit by God's glory. To be exposed to the fullness of God's glory would be too much for our reality to withstand and would instantly burn up everything that was exposed to a large amount of God's glory. There Is actually biblical verification for this.

2 Peter 3:7 KJV

But the heavens and the earth, which are now, by the same word are kept in store, reserved unto fire against the day of judgment and perdition of ungodly men.

2 Peter 3:10 KJV

But the day of the Lord will come as a thief in the night; in the which the heavens shall pass away with a great noise, and the elements shall melt with fervent heat, the earth also and the works that are therein shall be burned up.

This fervent heat that melts the elements is the fullness of God's glory that our reality will be exposed to when God removes the Torah/Law that covers our universe.

Therefore, one of the properties we are searching for in this veil that covers our universe is the ability to protect our current reality from the fervent heat that would come from the sudden exposure to God's glory.

We already went over how Adam's sin caused him to be cast out of the Garden of Eden that is in a different dimension, and placed under the Torah/Law. This is because sin is what caused us to fall or be separated from God's glory and the Law/Torah is literally what comes between us and our being fully exposed to God's glory. This gives us a new perspective when we look at Romans 3:23.

Romans 3:23 ESV

for all have sinned and fall short of the glory of God,

It is not just coincidence that the very next verse mentions the one who will eventually remove this veil that separates us from God's glory.

Romans 3:24 KJV

Being justified freely by his grace through the redemption that is in Christ Jesus:

So when we start our search the first thing we will need to look for is some type of physical matter that can shield us from the fervent heat that comes from the fullness of God's glory.

According to what we have already went over the Torah/Law contains all the information that is then projected to form our holographic reality. Therefore, the second thing we are looking for is some type of physical matter that is capable of storing a massive amount of information.

This seems to make our search a little more daunting because it will require the same physical substance to both shield us and be capable of storing massive amounts of information.

This search gets even more daunting when we consider that this information will have to be projected to form our reality.

This means that this physical substance will have to act like the silvered mirror we see used when making a hologram and also be the source of the information itself.

In the typical hologram the beam splitter or partially silvered mirror is separate from the information or object used to form the hologram. Of course a hologram that forms our reality is anything but typical.

Let's try and get a picture in our minds of what we are searching for. We know the information, or Law/Torah is described in the Bible as a veil the frames or surrounds our universe. This would likely be spherical because it frames our universe.

The Bible says that our universe is finite and describes it as a cloth that will be rolled up by Jesus at the end of this age.

Isaiah 50:3 KJV

I clothe the heavens with blackness, and I make sackcloth their covering.

The Bible also describes the earth as waxing old like a garment and the heavens vanishing like smoke when Jesus removes the veil that is the information that forms our holographic reality.

Isaiah 51:6 KJV

Lift up your eyes to the heavens, and look upon the earth beneath: for the heavens shall vanish away like smoke, and the earth shall wax old like

a garment, and they that dwell therein shall die in like manner: but my salvation shall be for ever, and my righteousness shall not be abolished.

If the universe is infinite modern science gives it a different shape, however, if the universe is finite modern science suggest it would take on the form of a sphere.

The following are excerpts from **https://www.space.com/24309-shape-of-the-universe.html**

If you could somehow manage to step outside of the universe, what would it look like? Scientists have struggled with this question, taking several different measurements in order to determine the geometry of the cosmos and whether or not it will come to an end. How do they measure the shape of the universe? And what have they found?

The shape of the universe depends on its density. If the density is more than the critical density, the universe is closed and curves like a sphere; if less, it will curve like a saddle. But if the actual density of the universe is equal to the critical density, as scientists think it is, then it will extend forever like a flat piece of paper.

Credit: NASA/WMAP Science team.

If the actual density of the universe is greater than the critical density, then it contains enough mass to eventually stop its expansion. In this case, the universe is closed and finite, though it has no

end, and has a spherical shape. Once the universe stops expanding, it will begin to contract. Galaxies will stop receding and start moving closer and closer together. Eventually, the universe will undergo the opposite of the Big Bang, often called the "Big Crunch." This is known as a closed universe.

Those excerpts shown from www.space.com admit that in a closed or finite universe the shape would be spherical.

They also say that they don't believe this is the case because they think the universe is eternal and hence the shape would be something other than spherical. As Christians we know God's word is absolute truth and therefore we know the universe is finite in both space and time, in which case both the Bible and modern science would show the universe being spherical.

So if we could see the universe or Torah/Law as an observer from the outside it would likely look something like the depiction given in the following drawing.

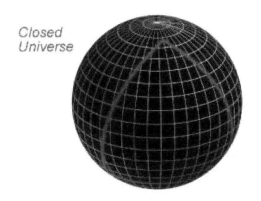

Keep in mind that what you are looking at would be the information that surrounds our universe, or the veil of darkness, and our reality would then be a projection of this that would end up in the center of this projected information.

So I will give a cut away depiction to get a better idea of what we are talking about. The black sphere in the center of the cut away drawing would represent our reality or universe.

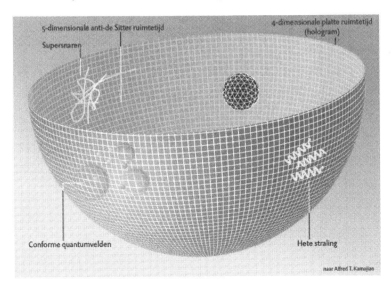

Now that we have an idea in our minds eye of what all this would likely look like let's search God's word for clues as to what type of physical matter this veil of information could be made from.

The Bible mentions this veil and what it is made out of during the creation account given for the age or reality we exist within.

Genesis 1:6-10 KJV

6 *And God said, Let there be a firmament in the midst of the waters, and let it divide the waters from the waters.*

7 *And God made the firmament, and divided the waters which were under the firmament from the waters which were above the firmament: and it was so.*

8 *And God called the firmament Heaven. And the evening and the morning were the second day.*

9 *And God said, Let the waters under the heaven be gathered together unto one place, and let the dry land appear: and it was so.*

10 *And God called the dry land Earth; and the gathering together of the waters called he Seas: and God saw that it was good.*

We can see that verse seven says that God divided the waters that are under the firmament from the waters that are above the firmament.

So we see that it does make reference to waters above the firmament.

Most people have assumed this is just making reference to the clouds we see in the sky that form rain. Some suggest that there was a canopy of water covering the sky before the flood of Noah and that God broke it open when He caused the flood to come.

Both Ideas are incorrect. To prove this we simply need to drop down to verses 14 through 19.

Genesis 1:14-19 KJV

14 And God said, Let there be lights in the firmament of the heaven to divide the day from the night; and let them be for signs, and for seasons, and for days, and years:

15 And let them be for lights in the firmament of the heaven to give light upon the earth: and it was so.

16 And God made two great lights; the greater light to rule the day, and the lesser light to rule the night: he made the stars also.

17 And God set them in the firmament of the heaven to give light upon the earth,

18 And to rule over the day and over the night, and to divide the light from the darkness: and God saw that it was good.

19 *And the evening and the morning were the*
fourth day.

In verse 14 it says "Let there be lights in the
firmament of the heaven". We know these lights
are The sun, moon, and stars. If the sun, moon,
and stars are in the firmament of the heaven and
verse seven says; "7 And God made the
firmament, and divided the waters which were

under the firmament from the waters which were
above the firmament".

 This verifies that there are waters above the
firmament that the sun, moon, and stars exist
within.

Amazingly this seems to indicate that the
Law/Torah that God placed over the universe is
made from water. But how can water possibly
store and retain vast amounts of information?

We will examine this in the next chapter.

BIBLE CODE (TORAH)   HE ENCODED THE TORAH, AND MORE

Bible Code (Torah) He encoded the Torah, and more

Chapter 10

Can Water Hold And Store Vast Amounts Of Information?

"The topic of memory in water has fascinated scientists for decades. Computer scientists have tried to understand how water can act in a manner similar to computer chips, potentially storing billions of bits of information in a teaspoon of water."

-www.aquatechnology.net

When most people think of water they think of what we use to hydrate our bodies, what we use to wash with, what we use to keep our lawns green, and even to help keep our car engines stay cool. The last thing most people would think of when contemplating the different uses of water would be using it for storing large amounts of information.

Remember, the real question we are asking ourselves is not do we currently have the technology to use water for storing information, but simply is water capable of storing a large amount of information?

Modern studies indicate that it is.

There is a difference between having a lot of information and being able to store a lot of information. In order to store and use information you must have some form of memory. So the first question we will address will be; does water have memory capabilities?

The Memory and secrets of water Prof. Dr. Bernd Kröplin

"When we now see in the drops of water that they talk to another, when information and mental energy seem to generate systematic changes, then it is worthwhile to at least look closer, because this could be the measurable beginning of that which we all know intuitively, that mind permeates matter and that thoughts manifest themselves in material structurings much more extensively than we now think possible. However, memory and information play a significant role in water, and these build a bridge from the immaterial to the material world.

These subtle phenomena are the ground of misunderstanding, and they can neither be studied nor detected by traditional experimental methods. Hence, we use a different approach:

we investigate the patterns that appear in a water drop after evaporation of the water and photograph them under a dark field microscope with a magnification between 40 and 400.

We can prove that the patterns correlate with information exposed to the water. For one experiment, the patterns are in most cases so similar that we can speak of reproducibility of the test.

The research in bio-resonance lead Prof. Kröplin to the study of water, as the basic element in the body and, hence, the one responsible for transporting much of the information thorough the different parts of the body at nano, micro and macro levels.

Understanding the way water collects and transports information was seen as the essential step to find out the complex behavior of our organs and their reaction to external agents.

Water "notes" the external influences that have acted upon it. This is especially important to us humans, as water makes up around 70% of our bodies. External factors that we expose ourselves to, be it music, electromagnetic radiation, ultra sound, x-ray or chemical substances, all have an impact on the water structure within our cells that can be seen under a microscope. Our research is based on observed phenomena and has a long way still to go."

Prof. Dr. Bernd Kröplin's studies indicate water has a form of memory, but there is admittedly a long ways to go in this research.

P.M Magazine wrote an article on Dr. Kroplin's research in July of 2005.

The following is an excerpt from that article.

"The pattern of the drop pictures," Kröplin is convinced, "are not coincidental." For instance structures of the drop pictures do change, when water is briefly exposed to the low electromagnetic field of a mobile phone. Afterwards the microscope pictures show exceptionally clearly visible structures, that are yet limited. "Water has remembered what happened", says Kröplin, "even though the mobile phone had been taken away."

P.M. Magazine – Welt des Wissens
Issue July 2005, p. 45-54

Though still in its infancy, the studies indicate that water does have a form of memory. Now the question is can water be used to store massive amounts of data?

The idea seems logical when we consider that our brains consist of over seventy percent water. This is also an area of research that is still in its infancy, however, it shows great promise and is being pursued by several different research teams.

Ryan Whitwam wrote an article on this research in 2014 that can be found at www.extremetech.com

The following is an excerpt from that article.

The liquid hard drive that could store a terabyte of data in a tablespoon of fluid

By Ryan Whitwam

A team of materials science researchers from the US may have just made the first breakthrough that could make so-called "soft matter" a viable data storage medium — at some incredible storage densities, too.

According to the new research, microscopic particles suspended in liquid could be used to encode the same 1s and 0s stored on solid hard drive platters today. They theorise that clusters of these particles could one day be used to store up to 1TB of data in one tablespoon of liquid hard drive.

Just how much information is in one terabyte? One terabyte is equal to approximately one thousand gigabytes.

This is hard to wrap one's mind around without breaking it down further by applying it to real world situations and seeing what we can get from one gigabyte.

1GB will get you:

- •3,500 emails with one word document attachment or

- •5,800 web page views or

- •68 5-minute YouTube videos

- •230 songs or 16 hours of music

- •1.5 hours of your favorite movie

The above isn't a total number. Each of those tasks would use 1GB by themselves, however, when you consider that one tablespoon of water can store one thousand gigabytes it starts to get pretty impressive.

1TB will get you:

- •3,500,000 emails with one word document attachment or

- 5,800,000 web page views or

- 68,000 5-minute YouTube videos

- 230,000 songs or nearly two years of non-stop music

- 1,500 hours of your favorite movie

That's a pretty impressive amount of information for one tablespoon full of water. Now consider how much water it would take to frame our entire universe. This is in fact what we are talking about with the biblical firmament as it is described in the Bible.

Even if this veil of water was one hundred miles deep it would still be far less than paper thin when compared to the immense size of the universe that it surrounds.

If you took all the water from all the oceans on earth it would not even be equal to one raindrop in the Pacific Ocean on scale to the amount of water we are talking about here.

The conclusion is that, as far as human comprehension is concerned, the amount of information contained in the water of the firmament would basically be infinite.

Theoretically water passes the test for being able to store and produce the information needed to sustain our holographic reality, but there is a lot more we need to consider here. The next question we need to ask ourselves is, would water provide enough protection as a barrier between us and the awesome glory of God? We will look into this in the next chapter.

○   5757 / 1997   □   FOR YOU THE ENCODED / HIDDEN SECRETS

◇   HE SEALED THE BOOK UNTIL THE TIME OF THE END

5757 / 1997. For You The Encoded/Hidden Secrets. He Sealed The Book Until The Time Of The End.

I believe we are living in the time of the end and the deepest secrets about the Bible code are being revealed to you as you read this book. We also see the date 1997 in this code. Interestingly, "The Bible Code" is a book by Michael Drosnin, first published in 1997.

Chapter 11
Water As A Shield Or Barrier

"Water is the driving force of all nature."

-Leonardo da Vinci

When it comes to God's glory it gets a little difficult to come up with any direct comparison and hence it's also difficult to decide just how much protection we would need to shield our fallen universe from the intense heat of His glory.

We can know by God's word that intense heat is one of the effects God's glory would, and will have on our fallen world once He removes the barrier between us and His glory/eternity, which is the Torah/Law/Scroll.

Isaiah 34:4 KJV

And all the host of heaven shall be dissolved, and the heavens shall be rolled together as a scroll: and all their host shall fall down, as the leaf falleth off from the vine, and as a falling fig from the fig tree.

The Bible gives a lot of literal clues as to what it is making reference to.

In this case the clue is, "as a scroll". It is not by chance that the Torah is copied onto a scroll. At this point all creation is suddenly exposed to the fullness of God's glory and the result will be everything being burned up by intense heat.

2 Peter 3:10 KJV

But the day of the Lord will come as a thief in the night; in the which the heavens shall pass away with a great noise, and the elements shall melt with fervent heat, the earth also and the works that are therein shall be burned up.

We know that God's glory clearly outshines the sun, however, the affects must be similar in some ways because the Bible compares the two, both in appearance and in the affects. We will start with appearance.

Matthew 17:1-2 KJV

1 And after six days Jesus taketh Peter, James, and John his brother, and bringeth them up into an high mountain apart,

2 And was transfigured before them: and his face did shine as the sun, and his raiment was white as the light.

So we can see that appearance of God's glory on Jesus' face is compared to the shining of the sun.

Obviously the sun is our source of light and heat for our current age and reality, however, when we enter the new age and reality God's glory will replace the sun as our light.

Isaiah 60:19 KJV

The sun shall be no more thy light by day; neither for brightness shall the moon give light unto thee: but the Lord shall be unto thee an everlasting light, and thy God thy glory.

Since the sun is a small example the Bible gives us to compare to God's glory we will also use the sun and its gamma rays to test the ability of water to act as a shield or barrier.

This process starts with nuclear fusion at the sun's core and by the time this reaches the sun's surface it is in the form of gamma rays. One thing that is easy enough to test is the ability of water to shield against nuclear radiation.

According to the following excerpt water is a very effective radiation shield and as little as seven centimeters of water can cut the radiation level in half.

"We know from the nuclear power industry that spent fuel storage pools are pretty safe places to be around, radiation-wise. They're actually safe to swim in, to a point, because they're serviced routinely by human divers. They just can't get too close to the spent fuel.

We use these pools for short-term storage because water is a really good radiation shield. How good? Well, according to a report on the topic prepared for the DoE back in 1977, a layer of water 7 centimeters thick reduces the ionizing radiation (rays and particles) transmitted through it by half (the remainder is captured or moderated to non-ionizing energy levels, mainly heat).

 Freshly discharged nuclear fuel puts out about 100,000 R/hour as measured from one foot away in air. At that rate, certain death is about 5 minutes' exposure and you'd fall into a coma in about 10."

Source:
https://space.stackexchange.com/questions/1336/what-thickness-depth-of-water-would-be-required-to-provide-radiation-shielding

So we can see that even a little water is a very affective shield against nuclear radiation. However, nuclear radiation, or even the sun itself, can in no way compare to the fullness of God's glory.

Therefore, I think it's safe to assume we would need an immense amount of water to act as a barrier or shield between our universe and God's glory.

We know God does not exaggerate and His word says that this barrier is a vast amount of water.

Psalm 29:3 HCSB

The voice of the LORD is above the waters. The God of glory thunders-- the LORD, above vast waters,

I think we can safely conclude that a vast amount of water would provide the perfect barrier to protect our fallen universe from the heat and intensity of God's glory.

But we know God's glory is immensely bright and that pure water is largely transparent and yet the Bible describes this veil of water as being dark and black.

Isaiah 50:3 KJV

I clothe the heavens with blackness, and I make sackcloth their covering.

Jeremiah 4:28 KJV

For this shall the earth mourn, and the heavens above be black: because I have spoken it, I have purposed it, and will not repent, neither will I turn back from it.

We also know that the Bible says this is a vast amount of water. So now the question is how much water would it take to completely block out the enormous amount of light that would be given off by God's glory? Since we can't use God's glory, for testing purposes we will, once again, use the sun.

If you have ever watched a TV show or movie that featured deep sea diving, such as The Titanic, then you know that it gets rather dark down in the great depths of the oceans. But how far would one need to go before you reached complete and total darkness?

The following excerpt provides the answer.

According to Water Encyclopedia Science and Issues; "The layer of the ocean where no light at all penetrates—over 90 percent of the entire ocean area on Earth—is called the aphotic zone, where depths are more than 1,000 meters (3,300 feet)."

So we can see that sunlight does not penetrate at all beyond 1,000 meters. As previously mentioned, God's glory is immensely brighter than the sun but we also know the Bible describes this Torah/veil of water information as being a vast amount of water.

We went over how even a thickness of one-hundred miles would be way less than paper thin when compared to the vastness of our universe. When we consider the size of the known universe the odds are in favor of this veil of water being much deeper than a mere one-hundred miles.

In any case, God knew exactly what was needed and this veil provides more than enough protection as a shield or barrier and He obviously created it deep enough to block the light of His glory, leaving this fallen universe in darkness.

We have discovered so far that water has a form of memory, water can hold vast amounts of information, water provides us with an excellent shield from intense heat, light, and radiation sources, and that water would be a veil of darkness at any reasonable depth. Now the only question is, would water provide the necessary components needed in order to form a very high-tech hologram?

We will tackle this issue in the next chapter.

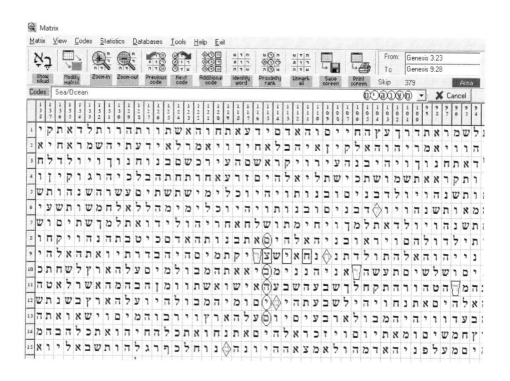

Sea/Ocean (**vertical ovals**) Partition/Barrier (**horizontal squares**) Splendour/Glory (**bucket shapes**) Heat (**diamonds**)

Matrix Odds = 1 chance in 1,851,542.656

Chapter 12

Does Water Provide The Necessary Components Needed To Form a Hologram?

"Examples of fractals are everywhere in nature. They can be found in the patterns of trees, branches, and ferns, in which each part appears to be a smaller image of the whole. They are found in the branch-like patterns of river systems, lightning, and blood vessels. They can be seen in snowflakes, seashells, crystals, and mountain ranges. We can even see the holographic and fractal-like nature of reality in the structure of the Universe itself, as the clusters of galaxies and dark matter resemble the neurons in our brain, the mycelium network of fungi, as well as the network of the man-made Internet."
-Joseph P. Kauffman

When one considers the necessary components needed to form a functional hologram water is probably one of the last things that would come to mind.

As we went over earlier, a hologram is made by shining a laser onto a partially silvered mirror that is called a beam splitter.

The beam splitter allows part of the laser to pass through the mirror while the reflected part of the laser gets directed to the object that is the information that will be stored on the holographic plate. Then both parts of the laser are redirected by other mirrors to meet up again at the holographic plate where the hologram is formed.

You probably noticed that there wasn't any mention of water in that process. What we need to keep in mind is that the description you just read is the process used to make a basic holographic still image.

If you wanted to form a projected hologram similar to what can be seen in the original Star Wars movie when they were on board the Millennial Falcon playing the holographic, life-like game, where Han Solo advised C-3PO to "always let the Wookie win", you would need a much more elaborate set-up than what is used to form the typical hologram.

With modern technology, projected, life-like, holograms are possible and in recent applications they are experimenting with water in different forms (liquid, vapor, and even frozen) and getting excellent results.

The following is an excerpt from an article written in 2014 that can be found at www.engadget.com

"It's 2014 and while we don't have flying cars just yet it looks like interactive holographic displays could be a reality rather soon. The not-so-cleverly-named Leia Display System (LDS) uses a combination of light, water-vapor and air to provide a transparent canvas for projected images while sensors track movement and touch inputs from users.

The videos we've embedded below show all manner of poking and prodding by users, a bit of MINORITY REPORT-style pinching and zooming things in mid-air and even using gestures to rotate and flick stuff out of the way. There's even a sample with a Mercedes sedan driving through the curtain and it "shattering" around the vehicle as it passes through."

An article at www.nature.com mentions that they are experimenting with liquid crystals for future 3D holographic movies.

"Holographic technology can produce three-dimensional images that can be seen without special eye-wear and without causing visual fatigue, but the images are usually static.

Takeo Sasaki and his colleagues at Tokyo University of Science used liquid crystals made from organic compounds to produce a dynamic hologram.

An electrical field applied to the liquid-crystal mixture alters how this medium bends, or refracts, the direction of incoming light.

The researchers sent coupled laser beams through the crystal mixture to generate a holographic image.

Although small and monochromatic, the hologram exhibited more than seven times the light amplification of previous attempts, and refreshed every 8 milliseconds — fast enough to produce a smooth holographic movie. Such a technique could be used for three-dimensional displays."

So we see that water and liquid crystals are showing great potential for use in future, life-like holographic projections.

By combining crystal chip holographic technology with 3D printers they are actually making solid physical objects. For now this technology is still in its infancy and the objects are only paper-clip size.

Here is an excerpt by Jamie Condliffe published on February 17, 2017 from www.technologyreview.com explaining this process.

-A bright-green laser flashes on, shining into a petri dish full of goo. From nowhere, the shape of a paper clip emerges—ghostly at first, then solid. Five seconds later the clip is fished out, cleaned up, and ready for use.

The basic principle here is an established 3-D-printing technique that uses lasers to cure a light-activated monomer into solid plastic. But unlike other approaches, which scan a laser back and forth to create shapes one layer at a time, this system does it all at once using a 3-D light field—in other words, a hologram. It could make 3-D printing far faster.

At the heart of the device that printed the paper clip is a holographic chip developed by Daqri, a startup that designs and builds augmented-reality devices out of laboratories in San Francisco and in Milton Keynes, U.K.-

The article goes on to tell how these holograms made from tunable crystals can be projected to assist in forming solid objects.

-The advantage of Daqri's chip, the company says, is that it can create holograms without the need for complex optics.

On a silicon wafer, a tiny grid of tunable crystals is used to control the magnitude and time delay, or phase, of reflected light shined at the surface of the chip from a laser.

Software adjusts the crystals to create patterns of interference in the light, resulting in a three-dimensional light field.

In experiments, the team has used the chip to create solid objects by projecting holograms into containers of various light-activated monomers.

It can currently make small objects, such as a paper clip, in about five seconds—a process that could take a normal 3-D printer several minutes.-

So we can see that both water and crystals, and different combinations of the two, are excellent for use in very advanced holographic technologies. I find it interesting that the Bible says that God's throne sits above this firmament of water that surrounds our universe and then in a different scripture reference it mentions the water that is before God's throne being a sea of glass that is like crystal.

Ezekiel 1:26 KJV

And above the firmament that was over their heads was the likeness of a throne, as the appearance of a sapphire stone: and upon the

likeness of the throne was the likeness as the appearance of a man above upon it.

Revelation 4:6 KJV

And before the throne there was a sea of glass like unto crystal: and in the midst of the throne, and round about the throne, were four beasts full of eyes before and behind.

Now we have established some amazing facts about water.

It happens to be the perfect material that meets all the requirements needed in the Biblical firmament.

1. Water can store vast amounts of information.

2. It has the memory so it can retain this information

3. It makes the perfect protective shield or barrier.

4. It provides all the necessary components needed to form a very high-tech hologram except for the actual laser itself.

God's glory takes the place of the laser in order to illuminate and project the information in the veil of water that frames our universe.

 God allowed a small beam of His glory, in the from of what we would call the theoretical white-hole, to enter our reality the moment He said; "let there be light."

We need to ask ourselves what the odds are that the Bible describes a firmament of water encompassing our universe and that water just happens to meet all the needed, and very extreme, requirements in order to fulfil all of the individual and very specific task?

The Bible describes Jesus as the Word, God as Light, and the Holy Spirit as Living Water. The Bible also describes the Three as One and forming the Holy Trinity.

All three work together to form our reality.

The Torah is the Word of God that frames our universe.

The Water is the material that the Torah is made from and it holds and stores the information.

The Light is the Glory of God that illuminates and projects the information.

All three become one to form our universe.

The Bible says that God made the heavens and the earth, but in other passages it describes teamwork and goes on to say that the team was one.

Genesis 1:1 KJV

In the beginning God created the heaven and the earth.

John 1:1 KJV

In the beginning was the Word, and the Word was with God, and the Word was God.

Jesus is the Word mentioned in John 1:1.

God is Light as mentioned in 1 John 1:5

1 John 1:5 KJV

This then is the message which we have heard of him, and declare unto you, that God is light, and in him is no darkness at all.

The Holy Spirit is Living Water as mentioned in John 7:37-39

John 7:37-39 KJV

37 In the last day, that great day of the feast, Jesus stood and cried, saying, If any man thirst, let him come unto me, and drink.

38 He that believeth on me, as the scripture hath said, out of his belly shall flow rivers of living water.

39 (But this spake he of the Spirit, which they that believe on him should receive: for the Holy Ghost was not yet given; because that Jesus was not yet glorified.)

All this information may seem like a stretch, especially for those who are not familiar with quantum physics, or who have had a different perception of how all this works that they have believed and held onto for years.

 I can certainly understand that, but I promise that everything we have covered will be proven beyond any doubt at the conclusion of this book to anyone who is willing to weigh out the overwhelming evidence presented when compared to the theories and conjecture that they have been conditioned to believe is true through many outlets such as public school systems and mainstream media.

In the Next chapter we will talk about how all this information would come together to form our reality and universe based on God's word and scientific analysis.

Hidden Light	אור גנוז
The Secret	הסוד
The Menorah	המנרה

2/38:31	ר ב י ב את א נ ו	2/38:30
2/40:24	ע ד י כ כ ה ה ש ל ח נ ע ל י ר	2/40:24
3/03:16	נ ה ו ה ק ט י ר מ ה כ ה	3/03:15
3/05:18	ו ה ו א ל א י ד ע	3/05:18
3/07:34	ו ל ח ק ע ו ל מ מ א ת ב נ י י ש ר א ל	3/07:34
3/09:18	ו י מ צ א ו ב נ י א ה ר נ א ת ה ד מ א ל	3/09:18
3/11:37	נ ב ל ת מ י ט מ א ו כ י י פ ל מ נ ב ל ת מ ע ל כ ל	3/11:36

Chapter 13

Our Holographic Universe By God's Design

"If you want to find the secrets of the universe, think in terms of energy, frequency and vibration."

-Nikola Tesla

We know that the universe is finite in both size and time references. As we went over earlier, a finite universe would be in the shape of a sphere.

The Bible describes a veil consisting of a vast amount of water that is surrounding our universe. Light cannot penetrate this veil, and hence, this veil would be black and leave our universe encased in darkness.

Isaiah 50:3 KJV

I clothe the heavens with blackness, and I make sackcloth their covering.

This water that forms the veil of darkness is not still like a pond, but is actually rushing water like you would find in a fast flowing river.

I will give the biblical evidence for this in the next chapter. The vast area of space between the water above and the earth's oceans below is what we know as outer-space.

Genesis 1:6-7 NLT

6 Then God said, "Let there be a space between the waters, to separate the waters of the heavens from the waters of the earth."

7 And that is what happened. God made this space to separate the waters of the earth from the waters of the heavens.

When one realizes that the "waters of the heavens" is actually making reference to the veil of darkness that frames our universe, and that the "space between" is what we know as outer-space, and then the other reference point is the "waters of the earth" we understand that what we have here is biblical verification of the Planck satellite findings; the earth is truly at the center of the universe.

Water can also act as the beam splitter or partially silvered mirror used to form a hologram. By observing how water interacts with the rays of light from the sun we can see that it absorbs part of the light and reflects part of it.

The water that forms the veil that surrounds our universe also contains the massive amount of information that is needed.

Unlike a typical hologram where the beam splitting mirror and the information, or object, are two separate things, with the high-tech hologram that forms our reality the beam splitter and the information are one and the same in the form of rushing water.

However, unlike the typical rushing water that almost seems chaotic, this rushing water has every part, at every moment, being intricately guided by God.

God is awesome beyond the imagination of man according to the Bible. What I find interesting is that one of the passages that mentions this also compares it to the heavens being higher than the earth.

Isaiah 55:8-9 KJV

8 For my thoughts are not your thoughts, neither are your ways my ways, saith the Lord.

9 For as the heavens are higher than the earth, so are my ways higher than your ways, and my thoughts than your thoughts.

I think it's safe to say that man will never completely comprehend the things of God in this lifetime but we can apply what we have learned in His word to what we know about holograms, and holographic projection, and get an idea of how creation works by God's design.

When God said "Let there be light" there was a sudden explosion of light that most people think

of as the Big Bang. Light was not created at that moment.

God simply opened a portal from eternity and let a sliver of His glory shine in. We can be certain of this because God is light and eternity is filled with His glory and therefore, light has always existed.

Eternity that is beyond our universe or "above the heavens" is lit by God's glory.

Psalm 8:1 KJV

O LORD our Lord, how excellent is thy name in all the earth! who hast set thy glory above the heavens.

We would know this small beam of God's glory as a white-hole. The biblical and scientific information that we went over indicates that this is likely located at the center of our Milky Way galaxy.

The veil of water that encircles our universe would absorb part of this light and reflect part allowing the light to interact and merge with the information/water and at the same time be projected towards the center of the spherical veil where everything would intersect to form our holographic reality.

This action would keep repeating as the light continued to reflect from different areas of the inside of the circle. Since the water is flowing it would constantly be redirecting massive amounts of information into the hologram causing it to form our living reality as we perceive it.

To say that I have over-simplified this explanation would be a very drastic understatement. But it does give us a basic idea of how it works that we can all wrap our minds around.

If you had God's view from eternity and were looking down on this veil of darkness that is made of water and surrounds our spherical shaped universe, it could possibly look something like this.

The Bible says that God spoke the universe into existence. When we speak the sound is made of vibrations at different frequencies that come from our vocal cords.

So one would think that creation would contain these frequencies and vibrations that would be caused by the voice of God speaking the Hebrew Torah.

"If you want to find the secrets of the universe, think in terms of energy, frequency and vibration."

-Nikola Tesla

If God used an audible voice during creation then one would think that we would somehow be able to hear God's voice within creation.

 In the next chapter we will use the word of God as our treasure map and see if we can actually find the audible voice of God.

בנואתשריכלתושאתתלכישדרכואתססמאותאצויבנוסברבתאשתולתכירשתואונב
מדסויבזןששמסמזבח◇הזיהוהויקראבשסמ◇הותוהיסעאאסברסמ◇הדהסרבאוסדה ורד
ופרעהאנשיסויישלוחאותואתתושתאלכאלרשלעתאויואתתויסולותויישלהאנעהרפו
אכהצעורואחברויכברהרויןרדרויכבאתכטולולרחביורועצהכא
אתכורלעמורושלשעעהשרהנהסנודרמארובעברבאוהשרעעעשלשורומלעדרכתא
נרוהסבעליברתאברסואמיעמאברסכינשבהאחירויאקרתחאתהן
ואתיענראשכלומאהרסיחולחלקסאהחרהדבריסההאלההיהיהדרה
אתסאברסויהייהשמשלבואןתרדמהנפלהעלאברסהותרהנהאימה
ברסלקולשריותקחשריאהשמןאסרומהגאתהרהמצריתשפחתהמהקקץ
שסיהוההדדברראליהאלראיכיאמרההההגסהלדסראיתאיתאחריי
עולסוההייתילהסלאלהיסוריאמראלהיסולאכרהסואתאההסתב
אבלשרההאשתךילדתלדבזןוקראתאתשמוריצחקותהקמ◇תיאתברריי

LIGHT, WATER, MATRIX, UNIVERSE

LIGHT (four diamonds on top) WATER (vertical ovals at center) MATRIX (three squares crossing "water") UNIVERSE (lower three diagonal circles connecting "matrix" to "water") Matrix Odds = 1 in 10,634,201.457

Chapter 14

Searching The Cosmos For The Voice Of God

"Wherever we are, God's in that moment, God's speaking to us, and if we've just got our ears open and our antennas up, there's no lack of inspiration. He's not silent. We just have to be listening."

-Steven Curtis Chapman

Since we are using the word of God as our map the first thing we need to do is see if the Bible gives us an idea of where we should begin looking on our quest to find, and hopefully hear, the voice of God.

I think Hebrews 11:3 will point us in the right direction.

Hebrews 11:3 KJV

Through faith we understand that the worlds were framed by the word of God, so that things which are seen were not made of things which do appear.

We can see that it says God's word frames the universe. This verifies the information that we have already went over. This is the location of the veil/Torah that surrounds our universe.

Now the big question is; is there anything in the Bible that would indicate there would be audible sound coming from this veil of darkness/Torah?

Believe it or not, there actually is and the answer is found in Psalm 19.

Psalm 19:1-11 KJV

1The heavens declare the glory of God; and the firmament sheweth his handywork.

2 Day unto day uttereth speech, and night unto night sheweth knowledge.

3 There is no speech nor language, where their voice is not heard.

4 Their line is gone out through all the earth, and their words to the end of the world. In them hath he set a tabernacle for the sun,

5 Which is as a bridegroom coming out of his chamber, and rejoiceth as a strong man to run a race.

6 His going forth is from the end of the heaven, and his circuit unto the ends of it: and there is nothing hid from the heat thereof.

7 The law of the Lord is perfect, converting the soul: the testimony of the Lord is sure, making wise the simple.

8 The statutes of the Lord are right, rejoicing the heart: the commandment of the Lord is pure, enlightening the eyes.

9 The fear of the Lord is clean, enduring for ever: the judgments of the Lord are true and righteous altogether.

10 More to be desired are they than gold, yea, than much fine gold: sweeter also than honey and the honeycomb.

11 Moreover by them is thy servant warned: and in keeping of them there is great reward.

So let's break it down and see what we discover starting with verse one.

1 The heavens declare the glory of God; and the firmament sheweth his handywork.

If we take verse one at face value it seems to say that the heavens literally speak out the glory of God and that the firmament, which is outer-space, shows us the work of God.

 It makes sense that the heavens would speak the glory of God since this is the location that

Hebrews 11:3 says the word of God is located at, and the work of God that we can observe would be the planets, stars, and galaxies etc.

Now let's examine verse two.

2 Day unto day uttereth speech, and night unto night sheweth knowledge.

It seems to be saying that each day speaks a language and that each night shows knowledge. This language would be ancient Hebrew and this knowledge would be the information within the Torah. This is confirmed in verse seven, but lets continue on to verse three for now.

3 There is no speech nor language, where their voice is not heard

We know that different languages are spoken throughout the earth. This indicates that God's voice (the Holy Trinity) can be heard and understood everywhere on earth, by Christians, through His Holy Spirit.

Verse four.

4 Their line is gone out through all the earth, and their words to the end of the world. In them hath he set a tabernacle for the sun,

This seems to be saying that the path of God's word reaches to the end of the world.

This would reaffirm the findings in verse three, that God's word can be heard everywhere on earth. It goes on to say that He set a tabernacle for the sun in them.

We know that the HolyTemple that comes from the heavens to earth in the next age is the New Jerusalem and it is referred to as a bride adorned for her husband.

At first glance it may seem strange that verse five describes this tabernacle as a Bridegroom.

5 Which is as a bridegroom coming out of his chamber, and rejoiceth as a strong man to run a race.

This is a biblical mystery that is solved when one realizes that the two become one through marriage. Jesus is the Head Cornerstone or capstone and the Church is the bride or body of Christ. The bride and groom together complete the pyramid shaped New Jerusalem.

Verse 6

6 *His going forth is from the end of the heaven, and his circuit unto the ends of it: and there is nothing hid from the heat thereof.*

As we covered earlier, The Lord exist in eternity which is beyond the veil of darkness or "the end of heaven." We also went over the fact that the Bible shows eternity is lit by God's glory which radiates immense heat.

"and there is nothing hid from the heat thereof."

Hence the reason that the elements melt with fervent heat when God removes the veil or rolls up the heavens as a scroll as described in 2 Peter 3:10, and also the reason this veil serves as a shield or barrier.

2 Peter 3:10 KJV

But the day of the Lord will come as a thief in the night; in the which the heavens shall pass away with a great noise, and the elements shall melt with fervent heat, the earth also and the works that are therein shall be burned up.

Let's move on to verse seven.

7 The law of the Lord is perfect, converting the soul: the testimony of the Lord is sure, making wise the simple.

This is the confirmation I mentioned after we went over verse two. The speech or knowledge that the heavens are declaring is the Law/Torah that frames the universe and contains all the information that forms our reality.

The second part of verse seven describes the Law as a testimony of the Lord. This testimony provides profound evidence of God's existence as you will witness at the end of this book.

Verses eight and nine.

8 The statutes of the Lord are right, rejoicing the heart: the commandment of the Lord is pure, enlightening the eyes.

9 The fear of the Lord is clean, enduring for ever: the judgments of the Lord are true and righteous altogether.

Verse eight and nine go on to further describe the Law/Torah as the statutes of the Lord, the commandments of the Lord, and the judgements of the Lord, all of which should lead us to fear the Lord.

And finally, verse ten.

10 *More to be desired are they than gold, yea, than much fine gold: sweeter also than honey and the honeycomb.*

This is saying that the wisdom and knowledge within the Law/Torah is more valuable than Gold

and hence the reason that we are truly on a treasure hunt!

On the next page you will notice a Bible code matrix. On one side the names Beloved, Bride, and Bridegroom were found and on the other side Jesus and Messiah are encoded along side Bridegroom.

The date 2009 can be found on one side and 2015 on the other side. The Bride (The Church) represents the Body of the New Jerusalem and the Bridegroom (Jesus Christ) represents the Head of the church or the Capstone. The Bride will be united with the Bridegroom when the raptures occurs.

The Dates come together to form a Pyramid with Rapture encoded at the center.

Could it be possible that one would also have to unite the dates by adding the 9, on 2009, to the 15, on 2015, to get 2024 as the year the rapture will take place?

I am not trying to make a prediction, but it is interesting.

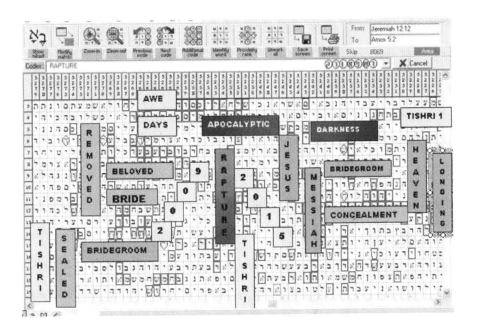

Chapter 15
How To Identify God's Voice

"Listen to the murmur of water and you'll hear Mother Nature.
Listen to the stillness beneath, and there you'll find God."

-Donald L. Hicks

According to what we have studied we know that we need to look towards the heavens in our search for God's voice. The problem is that "the heavens declare the glory of God" is not a very specific area in which to narrow down our search when we consider the size of the universe.

It would help if we actually knew exactly what we were listening for, but what does God's voice sound like?

If you asked one-hundred different people that question you would likely get one-hundred different replies based on several different factors like what religion they were raised with, if any, and what type of life experiences they have had that they relate to, or connect with God. Personally, I have heard everything from "it's a still quite voice from within" to "It sounds like thunder and you will know when you hear it."

We have read that the heavens declare His glory. We also know that His path is from the ends of the heavens, and that the heavens are covered with a vast amount of water.

Once again, the best place to search for answers when you want to discover the details about our Creator is in His word. So we will go to the word of God and see if we can narrow down our search to a more specific location and afterwards we will see if we can get a more detailed idea of what God's voice would sound like.

We already went over Psalm 19:1-11 which gave us a clue in verse six if you remember.

Psalm 19:6 KJV

His going forth is from the end of the heaven, and his circuit unto the ends of it: and there is nothing hid from the heat thereof.

So we know God and, the intense heat of His awesome glory, dwells in eternity beyond the heavens, or our universe.

That still doesn't narrow down the search too much as eternity seems like a very big place. Of course, space/time ceases to exist in eternity, so I guess applying size to eternity doesn't make much sense.

Let's try again.

Isaiah 13:5 KJV

They come from a far country, from the end of heaven, even the LORD, and the weapons of his indignation, to destroy the whole land.

Most agree that this verse is describing a judgement from God against Babylon. Regardless, it still gives the location of the Lord. He comes from the end of heaven, or in other words, the end of the universe.

That's still not very specific.

We went over how the veil of water that surrounds our universe would contain an infinite amount of information from man's perspective. We also discussed the fact that it would be impossible to gauge the depth of this vast amount of water, but even one-hundred miles deep would be paper thin when compared to the vastness of the cosmos.

Interestingly enough, when the NLT (New Living Translation) Bible explains God's infinite understanding and the fact that man can never completely comprehend it, it uses the word "depth."

Isaiah 40:28 NLT

Have you never heard? Have you never understood? The LORD is the everlasting God,

the Creator of all the earth. He never grows weak or weary. No one can measure the depths of his understanding.

We know the treasure hunt we are on is for the priceless wisdom and knowledge that is in God's word. Romans 11:33 confirms this and, once again, uses the word "depth" and mentions "judgments" (those without Christ are judged by the Law) in the KJV this time.

Romans 11:33 KJV

O the depth of the riches both of the wisdom and knowledge of God! how unsearchable are his judgments, and his ways past finding out!

So what's my point? There is almost always an easy to understand meaning in the plain text of God's word. But even the plain text has several layers of deeper wisdom and understanding beneath, which would give it "depth" in a manner of speaking.

I used Isaiah 40:28 and Romans 11:33 as an example of this because in the most basic way they explain that no man can ever fully grasp or reach the level of God's understanding. However, both verses also use the word depth in the translations given.

Depth also applies to water and we know the water above the heavens, that surrounds the universe, basically contains an infinite amount of information. To come to this understanding from the two verses given would be going deeper than what most would get from simply reading the plain text.

Some will think I am stretching things a little here. Remember, the information that forms the universe is in the veil of water that covers the heavens.

Now let's take a look at Psalm 136:5 in both the ESV and KJV.

Psalm 136:5 ESV

to him who by understanding made the heavens, for his steadfast love endures forever;

Psalm 136:5 KJV

To him that by wisdom made the heavens: for his mercy endureth for ever.

I am not saying that God's wisdom and understanding are limited to the information that forms our reality, but I am saying that when the Bible want's to give us an idea of God's wisdom and understanding it most often points us towards the making of the heavens. Why?

I think it's for two reasons.

#1 It's because within our reality there isn't anything that contains more information than the heavens because this is where God's word, in the form of the Torah, or the veil of water, is located.

#2 If we could ever penetrate the depths of this veil of water we would fully understand God as He fully understands us.

In other words, the "depth" is literally what separates us from deep understanding. Paul realized this.

Remember that our reality now is holographic and formed by light (God's glory) that contains the information after reflecting off the water/veil. In modern times they use Mirrors to make holograms. But in ancient times water was their mirrors.

"The first mirrors used by people were most likely to be a pool of water where they could observe their reflection and consider it magic."

Source: http://www.mirrorhistory.com/mirror-history/first-mirrors/

So not only did Paul realize that our reality is holographic, but he also realized that what forms our reality is also, ironically, the "depth" that

separates us from having complete understanding of God like He understands us.

1 Corinthians 13:12 NLT

Now we see things imperfectly, like puzzling reflections in a mirror, but then we will see everything with perfect clarity. All that I know now is partial and incomplete, but then I will know everything completely, just as God now knows me completely.

Since the universe is spherical, if we could reach the edge of the universe and we could dive into this pool of infinite information and swim to the other side we would end up in eternity with the Lord.

It is not by chance that the Bible says the Word (Jesus Christ) is the only way we can have a relationship with (know) the Lord. You will understand this better a little later in this book.

Now that we know there is deeper understanding the more time we spend searching out scripture (which always needs to be accompanied with prayer for the Lord's wisdom and guidance), let's go to Job 36:22-33 and peel back some layers.

Job 36:22-33 KJV

22 Behold, God exalteth by his power: who teacheth like him?

23 Who hath enjoined him his way? or who can say, Thou hast wrought iniquity?

24 Remember that thou magnify his work, which men behold.

25 Every man may see it; man may behold it afar off.

26 Behold, God is great, and we know him not, neither can the number of his years be searched out.

27 For he maketh small the drops of water: they pour down rain according to the vapour thereof:

28 Which the clouds do drop and distil upon man abundantly.

29 Also can any understand the spreadings of the clouds, or the noise of his tabernacle?

30 Behold, he spreadeth his light upon it, and covereth the bottom of the sea.

31 For by them judgeth he the people; he giveth meat in abundance.

32 With clouds he covereth the light; and commandeth it not to shine by the cloud that cometh betwixt.

33 The noise thereof sheweth concerning it, the cattle also concerning the vapour.

First of all I want to point out that peeling back layers, or looking deep into scripture, ALWAYS has to be done with the guidance of the Holy Spirit to ensure that the information we are extracting is actually deeper revelation of God's truth and not taking things out of context, or worse, making it up as we go along.

That being said, let's dig into these eleven verses, one-by-one and see what we find.

Verse 22.

Behold, God exalteth by his power: who teacheth like him?

Verse 22 starts by pointing out that nobody can come close to teaching like God. Through God's power and word we can get a much higher level of understanding. This verse is like a red flag signaling us to pay attention to the following verses where God will reveal some of His exalted teaching.

Verse 23.

Who hath enjoined him his way? or who can say, Thou hast wrought iniquity?

This is making reference to the veil of darkness that God placed over our universe that is the law and brings entropy. Remember, Jesus sets us free from the curse of the law by taking on our "iniquity."

Isaiah 53:6 KJV

All we like sheep have gone astray; we have turned every one to his own way; and the LORD hath laid on him the iniquity of us all.

Verse 24

24 Remember that thou magnify his work, which men behold.

This is a clue that the following verses will magnify God's work. In most cases when the Bible magnifies, or wants us to see how awesome God's work is, it points us towards creation in general and the heavens specifically.

There are examples of this throughout the Bible.

I will list a few.

Jeremiah 10:12 ESV

It is he who made the earth by his power, who established the world by his wisdom, and by his understanding stretched out the heavens.

Proverbs 3:19 ESV

The LORD by wisdom founded the earth; by understanding he established the heavens;

Isaiah 55:9 KJV

For as the heavens are higher than the earth, so are my ways higher than your ways, and my thoughts than your thoughts.

To further illustrate this point. I want to point a that Job 36:24 is literally saying " Remember that thou magnify his work", What is God's work?

Psalm 19:1 KJV

The heavens declare the glory of God; and the firmament sheweth his handywork.

The answer is the heavens, or firmament, which is another word for heavens.

Let's go to verse twenty five.

25 Every man may see it; man may behold it afar off.

Once again, this is making reference to the heavens, however, it is getting more specific. Depending on how good a man's eyes are and what time in history we are talking about, a different level of the heavens can be observed. Not all eyes are good enough to see most stars, however, even people with bad eyesight can usually see the Milky Way.

This is making reference to the cloudy formation that streams across the night sky that just about everyone with half way decent sight can observe.

We will begin to recognize this as the Milky Way as we read on.

The verses that follow make this more clear. Let's continue to verse twenty six.

26 Behold, God is great, and we know him not, neither can the number of his years be searched out.

This verse is just re-establishing the fact that no one understands the depth of how awesome God is. Man cannot comprehend eternity. God is from "everlasting to everlasting." He is the "Alpha and Omega."

Verse 27

27 For he maketh small the drops of water: they pour down rain according to the vapour thereof:We know the vapour that forms water as clouds.

That is what this verse is talking about in the plain texts. The Milky Way appears as a cloudy formation that spans the night sky, and this is the deeper meaning.

Verse 28

28 Which the clouds do drop and distil upon man abundantly.

Obviously, in the plain text, this is making mention of the rain that comes from clouds. But at the deeper level it is, once again, making reference to the Milky Way.

Verse 29

29 Also can any understand the spreadings of the clouds, or the noise of his tabernacle?

Now it's starting to get very specific at the deeper level. The cloudy formation that spreads acrossed the night sky is the Milky Way. If we remember what we went over earlier in the book we will understand that the tabernacle of the Bride is described as being in the heavens. Let's take another look at that.

Psalm 19:4-6 KJV

4 Their line is gone out through all the earth, and their words to the end of the world. In them hath he set a tabernacle for the sun,

5 Which is as a bridegroom coming out of his chamber, and rejoiceth as a strong man to run a race.

6 His going forth is from the end of the heaven, and his circuit unto the ends of it: and there is nothing hid from the heat thereof.

Based on that information we know that the spread out cloudy formation can only be the Milky Way which is in the heavens where the tabernacle of the Bride is located.

Job 29 ends with; *"the noise of his tabernacle."*

Remember that the whole point of this chapter is to narrow down our search of Bible and the heavens to a specific area so what we can discover the voice of God and maybe get an idea of what it sounds like.

I find it interesting that in Psalm 19 we discover that the heavens declare God's glory and that His tabernacle is also located there. In Job it seems to give us a more specific idea of where this sound and tabernacle come from, which is the Milky Way.

With that in mind, let's go to verse thirty.

30 Behold, he spreadeth his light upon it, and covereth the bottom of the sea.

God's glory is the light that is spread over the Milky Way and forms our reality. His glory enters our reality from eternity by a interdimensional portal that is located at the center of the Milky way.

We went over this earlier and the next few verses in Job will conform this. The scientific term for this would be a white-hole.

It is obviously important to remember the basics of how a hologram works if one is to reach a deeper understanding of our holographic reality by God's design. The white-hole is the light that shine on, and projects the information, which is the veil of darkness or the Torah/Law, which is a literal sea of information.

Hypothetically, if you could reach the edge of the universe and then dive into this sea of information and swim to the very bottom at the other side what would you find there? You would find the awesome glory of God covering the bottom of the sea right before you went interdimesional and entered eternity. Remember we are on verse 30. Let's look at it again.

30 Behold, he spreadeth his light upon it, and covereth the bottom of the sea.

Keep in mind that this sea is also the Law/Torah as we move on to verse 31.

31 For by them judgeth he the people; he giveth meat in abundance.

What does God use to judge the people that is also a curse or veil of darkness that was placed over our universe after the fall of Satan?

Galatians 3:10

"For as many as are of the works of the law are under the curse: for it is written, Cursed is every one that continueth not in all things which are written in the book of the law to do them."

It seems ironic, at first, that the the very one that represents the Law is the same one that sets us free from the curse of the Law, which is Jesus Christ, or the Living Word of God.

Galatians 3:13

"Christ hath redeemed us from the curse of the law, being made a curse for us: for it is written, Cursed is every one that hangeth on a tree:"

The Law represents the perfection of God. Jesus is the mirror image of God and in fact He and God are one and the same. Jesus is also the mirror image of the Law, which is the Torah, or Word of God. Jesus and the Law are one and the same, and both are perfect.

We can go right back to Psalm 19 to confirm this.

Psalm 19:7 KJV

The law of the LORD is perfect, converting the soul: the testimony of the LORD is sure, making wise the simple.

There is only one name in heaven and earth that can convert your soul and His name is Jesus Christ.

Jesus represents the pyramid/tetrahedron at the quantum level that our holographic reality starts with, which is the head stone or capstone (the head of all four corners on a pyramid) on the New Jerusalem.

Acts 4:11-12 KJV

11 This is the stone which was set at nought of you builders, which is become the head of the corner.

12 Neither is there salvation in any other: for there is none other name under heaven given among men, whereby we must be saved.

This is explained in a lot more amazing detail in my book "The Matrix Code and The Alien Agenda."

Once we accept Jesus Christ as our personal Savior God does not see our sin anymore.

From that point on His Holy Spirit dwells inside us and God only sees the righteousness of Jesus Christ when He looks at us.

Isaiah 1:18 KJV

Come now, and let us reason together, saith the LORD: though your sins be as scarlet, they shall be as white as snow; though they be red like crimson, they shall be as wool.

Psalm 103:12 KJV

As far as the east is from the west, so far hath he removed our transgressions from us.

Now let's get back to Job 36:31

31 For by them judgeth he the people; he giveth meat in abundance.

Jesus is the Law, but He is also the Bread of Life.

John 6:35 KJV

And Jesus said unto them, I am the bread of life: he that cometh to me shall never hunger; and he that believeth on me shall never thirst.

That's why Jesus commands us to feed His sheep with His word.

Now let's move on to verse 32.

32 With clouds he covereth the light; and commandeth it not to shine by the cloud that cometh betwixt.

In the plain text this is easy to understand as we know the clouds come between us and the sun. But at the deeper level it is explaining exactly what occurs at the center of the Milky Way Galaxy.

Scientist cannot get a good look at the Milky Way's center because of the thick cloudy looking formation of stars that covers this area. In other words, the clouds cover the light.

The following is an excerpt from http://www.aenigmatis.com/astronomy/find/sagittarius.htm

-*Sagittarius* is home to a wealth of interesting astronomical objects. This is mainly due to the fact that, when we look at *Sagittarius*, we are looking towards the centre of our own *Milky Way Galaxy*, where the density of stars and gas/dust clouds (*nebulae*) is greatest. Indeed, the actual centre of the galaxy is located at the South-eastern corner of the constellation, hidden behind dark clouds of interstellar dust, close to the boundary with *Scorpius*. Under dark skies, the *Milky Way* glows distinctly in the region of *Sagittarius*-

You probably noticed that even in this excerpt the dense star formation that blocks our view from the

Milky Way's center is referred to as "dark clouds".

Scientist will go against the vast amount of obvious evidence (some of which we went over earlier in the book) that shows a white-hole at the galaxies center and they will call it a black hole because they have been told and taught that white-holes likely don't exist and that black-holes are common, and most likely always, in the center of spiral galaxies.

Even atsro Bob believes that there is a black-hole at the galactic center, because that's what astro Bob has been conditioned to believe through the modern education system and main stream media. Yet, Bob mentions that if you could remove the cloudy star formations the center of the Milky Way would be so bright that it would cast shadows at night.

Here is what Bob has to say pertaining to this.

-Though the center remains hidden, large chunks of the Milky Way hover like clouds against the black sky. Every puffy piece is comprised of billions of distant stars the light of which blends together to form a misty haze. Here and there are smaller knots. These are individual gas clouds called nebulae and bright star clusters.

 A pair of 40-50mm binoculars will show many of these wonders and countless fainter stars plainly. If we could magically remove the dust between us and the galactic center, the rich intensity of stars in the Sagittarius direction would be bright enough to cast shadows at night.-

Source: astrobob.areavoices.com

The following are a couple excerpts from Wikipedia on the center of the Milky Way or Sagittarius A.

-**Sagittarius A** or **Sgr A** is a complex radio source at the center of the Milky Way. It is located in the constellation Sagittarius, and is hidden from view at optical wavelengths by large clouds of cosmic dust in the spiral arms of the Milky Way.

It consists of three components, the supernova remnant **Sagittarius A East**, the spiral structure **Sagittarius A West**, and a very bright compact radio source at the center of the spiral, **Sagittarius A***. These three overlap: Sagittarius A East is the largest, West appears off-center within East, and A* is at the center of West.-

Aenigmatis can't explain why...-the *Milky Way* glows distinctly in the region of *Sagittarius*-.

Bob thinks it is due to...- the rich intensity of stars-.

But it is actually way too bright to be caused by star clusters.

Wikipedia doesn't understand it either, so they admittedly use conjecture to explain it. Before I post the excerpt of their explanation Let's get the exact definition for "conjecture".

Merriam-Webster

Definition of **CONJECTURE**

1a : inference formed without proof or sufficient evidence
b : a conclusion deduced by surmise or guesswork

Here's the excerpt trying to explain the white-hole from Wikipedia.

Sagittarius A East

-This feature is approximately 25 light-years in width and has the attributes of a supernova remnant from an explosive event that occurred between 35,000 and 100,000 BCE. However, it would take 50 to 100 times more energy than a standard supernova explosion to create a structure of this size and energy.
 It is conjectured that Sgr A East is the remnant of the explosion of a star that was gravitationally compressed as it made a close approach to the central black hole.-

What they won't tell you is that they really don't have any evidence and they are just guessing (pun intended as that's the definition of conjecture) because they have no idea why the center of our Milky Way is so bright and behaves like, well, like the white-hole that it is.

And lastly, verse thirty-three.

33 The noise thereof sheweth concerning it, the cattle also concerning the vapour.

In the plain text this is telling how the cattle benefit from the rain. At the deeper level it is saying that the "noise" will show or give the evidence confirming the Law/Torah that is made from water and refrenced in verse twenty-three of this chapter. This is our first clue that the water is moving. We can easily hear rushing water but still water is silent.

Could this noise be the voice of the Lord that we are searching for? If so this would mean that we should probably search the southern skies and the center of our galaxy for the source of God's voice.

At first glance, this seems to contradict other parts of the Bible that clearly indicate heaven is in the north.

I will present the evidence that seems contradicting, but before I do I want to give a quote from Dr. Chuck Missler regarding when we seem to find a contradiction in the Bible.

"Whenever you find an apparent contradiction in the Biblical text, we should rejoice! It may be what the rabbis call a remez: a hint of something deeper. It's like a signpost saying, "Dig here! A treasure is hidden here." -Chuck Missler

Now let's look at these seemingly contradicting verses that seem to say heaven is in the north.

Lucifer in his rebellion (when he tried to make himself equal to God) mentions heaven and the stars of God (the angels, or heavenly host) being in the north.

Isaiah 14:13 KJV

For thou hast said in thine heart, I will ascend into heaven, I will exalt my throne above the stars of God: I will sit also upon the mount of the congregation, in the sides of the north:

Psalm 48:1-2 also seems to say heaven is in the north.

1. Great is the Lord, and greatly to be praised in the city of our God, in the mountain of his holiness.

2. Beautiful for situation, the joy of the whole earth, is mount Zion, on the sides of the north, the city of the great King.

So how can the tabernacle of the Lord, which seems to be the New Jerusalem, be in the south as Job indicates and the the city of God (which is the New Jerusalem) be in the north as Psalm 48:1-2 indicates?

Does this mean we have reached a dead end on our treasure hunt to solve the Bible Code and, by doing so, literally hear the voice of the Lord?

There is only one way that the New Jerusalem can be in the North and the South and everything still make sense. Like Chuck Missler said, this is a remez; "a hint of something deeper. It's like a signpost saying, "Dig here! A treasure is hidden here."

We established earlier that creation under the veil during our current age happened when God said; *"Let there be light."*

At this time light shot forth from the center of the Milky Way and illuminated the information. The information was the Word of God/Law that frames our universe and represents Jesus Christ.

The perfect one, and the only one, who converts our souls is Jesus Christ.

Psalm 19:7 KJV

The law of the LORD is perfect, converting the soul: the testimony of the LORD is sure, making wise the simple.

The Word of God, the Perfect law, and Jesus Christ are one and the same.

The information is contained in vast rushing waters, or moving/living waters. The veil is made from a vast amount of flowing water and represents the Holy Spirit.

John 7:37-39 KJV

37 In the last day, that great day of the feast, Jesus stood and cried, saying, If any man thirst, let him come unto me, and drink.

38 He that believeth on me, as the scripture hath said, out of his belly shall flow rivers of living water.

39 (But this spake he of the Spirit, which they that believe on him should receive: for the Holy Ghost was not yet given; because that Jesus was not yet glorified.)

This water is the Holy Spirit.

" But this spake he of the Spirit."

The Light or God's glory shines on and illuminates the Law/The Torah/The Word/ Jesus Christ, which is the information/mirror and reflects the glory. Then the Holy Spirit communicates this and disperses it out to the correct areas at the perfect time.

But is there any biblical verification that the law/Torah could be a mirror?

James 1:23-25 ESV

23 For if anyone is a hearer of the word (the Law-Author's note) and not a doer, he is like a man who looks intently at his natural face in a mirror.

24 For he looks at himself and goes away and at once forgets what he was like.

(what do we look like? Jesus Christ! We are made in the image of God-Author's not)

25 *But the one who looks into the perfect law (Jesus Christ-Author's note), the law of liberty, and perseveres, being no hearer who forgets but a doer who acts, he will be blessed in his doing.*

The "perfect law" is the mirror!

What did Jesus say?

John 10:30 KJV

" I and my Father are one. "

This explains how God can literally be in the south, shining His glory, and the Law/Jesus Christ in the north reflecting His glory, then the Holy Spirit dispersing His glory, to create one reality/universe.

All three as one form our holographic reality.

The one who communicates the message, or information, is the Holy Spirit.

The water, or voice that represents God is the Holy Spirit.

Therefore, God's voice, in the form of the Holy Spirit, would sound like a vast amount of rushing water. But is this biblically verfied?

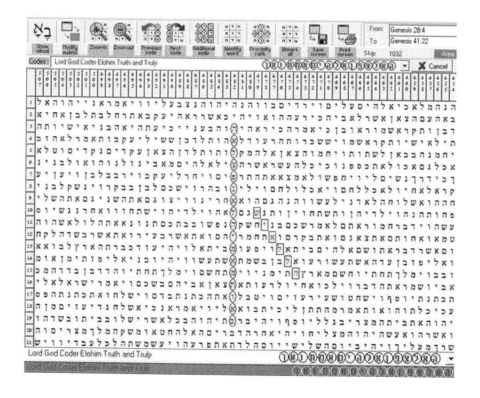

"Lord God Coder Elohim, Truth and Truly"

Chapter 16

Biblical Proof Of The Voice of God

"But the Helper, the Holy Spirit, whom the Father will send in my name, he will teach you all things and bring to your remembrance all that I have said to you."

-John 14:26 ESV

Now we know that the Holy Spirit is the Living Water in the veil. He is rushing waters and speaks God's will to us. Therefore, the voice of the Lord should sound like rushing waters. But is there any biblical verification for this?

Psalm 29:3 KJV

The voice of the LORD is upon the waters: the God of glory thundereth: the LORD is upon many waters.

Revelation 1:15 KJV

And his feet like unto fine brass, as if they burned in a furnace; and his voice as the sound of many waters.

Ezekiel 43:2 KJV

And, behold, the glory of the God of Israel came from the way of the east: and his voice was like a noise of many waters: and the earth shined with his glory.

Relevation 14:2 BSB

And I heard a sound from heaven like the roar of rushing waters and the loud rumbling of thunder. And the sound I heard was like harpists strumming their harps.

So we can see that it is biblically verified that the voice of the Lord sounds like a vast amount of rushing waters.

Now we know what it is,water. We know what it sounds like, rushing water. We know where it is located, it frames our universe.

When David said, "the heavens declare the glory of God" he gave the location in His very next statement, "The firmament showeth His handiwork."

The technology to listen to the heavens did not exist during David's time.

David was inspired by God when he made that statement. All of God's Word is inspired and Living!

Hebrews 4:12 ESV

For the word of God is living and active, sharper than any two-edged sword, piercing to the division of soul and of spirit, of joints and of marrow, and discerning the thoughts and intentions of the heart.

Since we have identified what our treasure is, where it's located, and exactly what it sounds like, let's go there and see what we find.

At this point it is necessary that you follow my instructions to the letter so that you can fully appreciate and enjoy the treasure. You will need a computer and an internet connection.

The first thing you should do is listen to a large flow of rushing water so that you have the exact sound fresh in your mind in order to be able to verify with absolute certainty when you hear the voice of the Lord.

I am going to give you the location of a YouTube video that allows you to listen to the all natural, un-edited, sound of the Niagara Falls. Basically, any large flow of water will work, but I think this is an excellent example.

Please go to YouTube and type in;

"Sounds of Niagara Falls (Niagara Whirlpool, Horseshoe Falls, American Falls) HD1080".

Now that you have the exact sound that we are looking for fresh in your mind I am going to tell you where you can go to literally hear the sound of God's voice.

It is in the exact location that God's word said it would be and also in the exact location it would need to be to form our reality.

It is located beyond the stars that are in the firmament in the cosmic background!

Keep in mind that this will sound like it is in the distance because it is.

Now please go back to YouTube and type in; "Cosmic Background Radiation Ambient Noise (12 Hours)"

Forget everything that you have been conditioned to believe and be honest with yourself. What are you hearing? You are hearing the sound of a vast amount of rushing water in the distance of the universe.

You are listening to the voice of the Lord!

It is in the exact location that God's word said it would be and it is making the exact sound that God's word said it would make.

This is profound and amazing evidence that God exist and He is exactly who He claims to be, the Creator of the universe.

Of course, modern science and un-believers will try to explain this away.

We know that modern technology is needed, using radio telescopes, in order to hear this, but so did the Creator of the universe when he mentioned it over 2,000 years ago in His word.

For those of you who may still be doubting the observation that you just made with your ears, hopefully, you will believe another observation that you can make to confirm these findings using your eyes.

This will be an observation of deep space to confirm that water does in fact "frame" our universe.

I would like to show you the results of the Millennium Run project.

The Millenium Run used more than 10 billion particles to trace the evolution of the matter distribution in a cubic region of the Universe over 2 billion light-years on a side.

It kept busy the principal supercomputer at the Max Planck Society's Supercomputing Center in Garching, Germany for more than a month.

This is a photo of their results that is placed directly below water.

Upon viewing these photos you will have verified the biblical findings with both your hearing and sight.

WATER

UNIVERSE

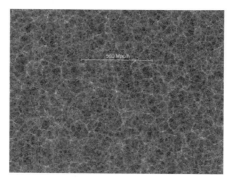

Some of you will claim that the sound of rushing water is simply white noise given off by radio telescopes. Modern science would have us believe that this is simply the aftermath of the Big Bang. So let's take a closer look at this and see what the evidence points to.

When you tune your radio to a certain frequency you will pick up whatever sound is being made at the source of the frequency that you are tuned to. For example, if I tune my radio to 94.3 FM I will hear the voice of the DJ or the sound of the music that is playing at the radio station that operates at 94.3 FM.

The radio frequencies simply transmit the sound that is given from the source of said frequency. If I am not tuned to any frequency I will get "white noise". If I am watching this on a television set this will appear as "snow" and it will sound exactly like rushing water.

The untuned radio or TV simply goes back to its natural frequency which then picks up the natural sound at the source of this frequency which is rushing water. This rushing water contains all the information that is then projected to form our holographic reality.

The "snow" that you see on your television set is

simply the scrambled holographic information that forms our reality. Our brains are tuned to the correct frequency so what we can see, hear, taste, touch, feel, and smell this projected information in the form of what we perceive as reality.

This conclusion can also be visually verified. First, let's take a look at the scrambled information as it is seen on a holographic plate. This is how it appears before the laser is shined onto it and before the holographic image is formed.

Holographic Plate

Now let's take a look at the scrambled information that forms our reality. This is how it appears before our brains process it and before we see it as our reality.

Since this is not tuned to any certain frequency the sound that we will hear is the default sound given off by the source which is the rushing water that contains the information that forms our holographic reality.

You can go to YouTube and type in "TV static noise (snow screen), white noise" and listen to this yourself. Then compare what you are hearing to the cosmic background noise. Afterward compare both of the aforementioned to the sound of Niagara Falls.

The conclusions in this book have been verified in every possible way short of actually traveling to the edge of the universe and placing your hand in this water. For those of you who can break free of the false information that you have been fed all your life through school and mainstream media this information will verify that God's word is one hundred percent true.

God's word says that He loves us so much that He sent His Son, Jesus Christ, to come into our fallen universe and pay a debt that is ours.

We sinned. We are fallen, and yet having a relationship with us meant so much to Him that he was willing to die and pay the price for us. He conquered death and rose again on the third day.

Most people don't consider exactly what Jesus went through on our behalf. Most of us have heard that He died on the cross. This in itself is a horrifically painful death that is drawn out over a long time period and involves a lot of pain and suffering. However, there is more that Jesus went through for us that most do not consider.

I want you to think about the worst thing you have ever done in your life that nobody, or very few know about. Something that you would be very ashamed of, and embarrassed about, if it was ever shown or revealed publicly. We all have skeletons in our proverbial closets of life that we would really like to keep hidden.

Now consider this; Jesus literally took all the sinful and shameful acts of man, from the beginning, until the end of our reality, upon Himself and then showed them to Father God.

 It was so aweful that God turned His head away and the day was plunged into darkness. Emotionally, in the flesh, this made Jesus feel like he had been forsaken.

Mathew 27:46 KJV

46 And about the ninth hour Jesus cried with a loud voice, saying, Eli, Eli, lama sabachthani? that is to say, My God, my God, why hast thou forsaken me?

God never left His Son, but this gives us an idea of what Jesus was feeling emotionally. The emotional suffering He endured on our behalf was on par with the physical suffering. God's great love for us is beyond our comprehension.

John 3:16-17 KJV

16 For God so loved the world, that he gave his only begotten Son, that whosoever believeth in him should not perish, but have everlasting life.

17 For God sent not his Son into the world to condemn the world; but that the world through him might be saved.

So how can you receive this free treasure of eternal life that God freely offers? The answer can be found in Romans 10:9.

Romans 10:9 KJV

That if thou shalt confess with thy mouth the Lord Jesus, and shalt believe in thine heart that God hath raised him from the dead, thou shalt be saved.

You don't have to wait. The Bible says to come as you are. You can pray and ask Jesus to come into your life as your Lord and Savior today!

מ ש ו ש ב א
מ ש י ח י נ ש א מ ר ם

דתיאתכמסח	ה :	ד	ה	**Joy**
קיסומשפט	ה :	ד	ה	
יסכאשרצו	ה :	ד	ה	**is coming,**
ניירוראל	ה :	ד	ה	
רילעשותכ	ה :	ד	ה	**Messiah**
ובקרבהאר	ה :	ד	ה	
עאשראתמב	ה :	ד	ה	**will rise**
איסשמהלר	ה :	ד	ה	
שתהושמרת	ה :	ד	ה	**on high**
סועשיתמכ	ו :	ד	ה	
יהואהכמת	ו :	ד	ה	
כמובינתכ	ו :	ד	ה	
סלעינ יהע	ו :	ד	ה	
מיסאשריש	ו :	ד	ה	
מעורןאתכל	ו :	ו	ה	
החקיסהאל	ו :	ד	ה	
הואמרורק	ו :	ד	ה	
עמחכמונב	ו :	ד	ה	
וןהגריהג	ו :	ד	ה	

Conclusion

God Has a Sense of Humor

"Professing themselves to be wise, they became fools,"

-Romans 1:22 KJV

Modern man has been listening to the cosmic background noise using radio telescopes since 1937 for a sign of inteligent life.

They have literally been listening to the voice of God for eighty years searching within it for some signal that would let them verify that there is inteligent life in the universe.

If this isn't the ultimate irony I don't know what is.

The Bible Code has been solved. Now we know why they find the past, present, and future when they search in the 2D written Torah. The Torah is the source code that forms our reality and the literal spoken Word of God that frames our universe!

Now the question is; what will man do with this information?

Now that they know what the Bible code is what would happen if they were to use modern computer technology to decipher and combine this information with the 2D Torah? What kind of amazing discoveries will be made and what will they do with this information once they access it?

These were some of the questions and concerns I had when writing this book. I prayerfully came to the conclusion that the amazing verification this provides, both for those who are searching for the Lord, and for us who are already saved, is worth the risk. The bottom line is that God is in complete control.

As for me, I will never listen to rushing water again without thinking of the voice of our Lord.

God Bless!

Tracy Yates

Daniel 12:4 KJV

But thou, O Daniel, shut up the words, and seal the book, even to the time of the end: many shall run to and fro, and knowledge shall be increased.

וְרָאָנֹכִי כִּמְנֻוּהָאֶתְכֶמְעוֹלֹתִיכֶם
שְׁמַחְתֶּמְלִפְנֵי יְיהֹוָהאֱלֹהֵיכֶמַא
לוֹחֶלְקֻוּוֹחֲלָהָאֶתְכֶמַהַשְׁמֶרלְךָ
וּבָטֵיךָשָׁמַעֲלֵהֹעֲלֹתִיךָ וְשָׂמַתַּעַ
יְהֵיךָאֲשֶׁרתַןלְדָּבְכָלְשִׁעֲרֵיךָהַ
וְיֹסֹלֹאתוֹלְלָאֶכֹלֹבַשִׁעֲרֵיךָמֶעִ
.תֵיךָוְתֹרוּמַתֹיָדְךָכִּיאֹמַלְפְנֵי י

⬭ **Bible Code**

▢ **sealed before God**

Acknowledgments

I would like to think my Lord and Savior, Jesus Christ, for giving me the wisdom, understanding, and discernment needed to write this book.

I do not deserve the credit for the amazing discoveries and information contained in this book. This information is revelation from the Lord in the most literal sense. Just writing this book took a step of faith as I did not have all the answers or needed info when I started. I felt like God was telling me to write this book and so I did.

The only way I can describe the amazing journey that God took me on while writing this book would be to compare it with the 1984 movieThe Never Ending Story where the lead character, Bastian, sneaks an old book out of a bookstore and begins reading it, once he gets home, after hiding away in the attic.

The story seems to come alive as he is reading it.

This was how it felt for me as I wrote this book. I felt like God took me on an amazing journey and I was just along for the ride. Therefore, God deserves all the credit for these amazing discoveries.

Made in the USA
Columbia, SC
29 June 2022

62476266R00115